The ultimate GOLF trivia book

MIKE TOWLE

Rutledge Hill Press®

Nashville, Tennessee

A Division of Thomas Nelson, Inc.

www.ThomasNelson.com

Published by Rutledge Hill Press, a Division of Thomas Nelson, Inc., P.O. Box 141000, Nashville, Tennessee 37214.

Cover photos by Phil Sheldon, Photodisc, and Art Today

Cover design by Timothy Holland

Typography by Roger A. DeLiso, Rutledge Hill Press®

Library of Congress Cataloging-in-Publication Data:

Towle, Mike.
  The ultimate golf trivia book / Mike Towle.
    p. cm.
  Includes bibliographical references (p. 253).
  ISBN 1-55853-749-X (pb)
  1. Golf--Miscellanea.   I. Title.
GV967.T56   1999
796.352--dc21   99-13351
                                                       CIP

Printed in the United States of America

02 03 04 05 06 — 8 7 6 5 4

To Holley and Andrew,
for their patience, love, and understanding.

TABLE OF CONTENTS

Front Nine

Back Nine

ACKNOWLEDGMENTS

I owe a big bucket of thanks to all the folks who steadied me all the way to the nineteenth hole.

My wife Holley and son Andrew gave me the freedom during my "free time" from a full-time job to spend the better chunk of six months putting this thing together.

To Michelle Noel and her staff at the Cumberland University library in Lebanon, Tennessee: thanks for all your cheerful help and access to hundreds of issues of golf magazines.

I am grateful to a number of my fellow golf journalists and friends for helping me "de-bug" the manuscript. Matt Rudy, Michael Arkush, Steve Eubanks, Tim Rosaforte, Melanie Hauser, Joe Passov, and Curt Sampson were generous with their time and knowledge. Thanks, David Feherty, for knocking a three-iron stiff with your foreword. Thanks, too, to Jim Nantz, and, again, Curt Sampson, for giving this book a nice shot in the arm.

I thank the following cohorts for their support over the years: Dave Metcalf, Leonard Parent, Kirk Faryniasz, Gene Frenette, John Cunavelis, Chuck Pearce, John Fineran, Bob Best, Roger Valdiserri, John Heisler, Madonna Kolbenschlag, Ted Robinson, Mark Arminio, Fred Herbst, Paul Stevenson, Ray O'Brien, Tim Bourret, Bob Donnelly, Greg Jones, Jack Raudy, Terry White, Rhonda Glenn, Ron Coffman, Brett Avery, Jim Herre, Mark Godich, Bill Kraftson, Larry Moody, Mark Brooks, Larry Mize, Scott Simpson, Kathy Guadagnino, Suzanne Strudwick, Bruce Raben, Steve Meyerhoff, Ed Choate, Bob Hille, Ellen Thornley, Peter Alfano, Mike Corcoran, John Poinier, Frank Deford, Vince Doria, Mike Patterson, Domingo Ramirez Jr., O. K. Carter, Mark Witherspoon, Jimmy Burch, Wendell Barnhouse, Jeff Rude, Steve Pate, Al Tays, Ron Sirak, Lisa Vannais, Al Barkow, George Allen, Scott Waxman, Jim Donovan, Rich Skyzinski, Kevin O'Connor, and Larry Dorman.

Phil and Gill Sheldon were quick to shower me with photos from which to pick and choose. Thanks, too, to the Library of Congress Photographic Services, the LPGA, the PGA Tour, Jon Bradley, and Byron Nelson.

I thank my family for being there through thick and thin: Dad (Bill), Mom (Anne), Kathy, Andy (in loving memory), Betsy, and Jay. My grandfather, Roy Carpenter, is well into his nineties and a lover of golf, too. Terry Baker, Mark Ingalls, Al Esty, Ovila Smith, Wayne and Glenn Singleton, Brian Moroney, Terry O'Reilly, and Bruce Bullock have been great golf partners over the years.

Thanks, too, to the entire team at Rutledge Hill Press for making a go of this.

Finally, and most of all, I thank Jesus Christ for the free pass.

FOREWORD

As an announcer, I find this book to be a godsend. Finally, we can throw away all those butt-numbingly boring, who-gives-a-rat's-tooth stat sheets about total driving (whatever the hell that means), putts per round, and sand saves.

Now, while some player is taking forever to line up a putt that you or I could just as easily miss in half the time, we can be spouting some actually interesting golf trivia at the general public. And believe me, golf is a trivial pursuit if ever there was one.

The point is, in the time that it has taken for you to read this far, you could have, by simply skipping this entire mindless foreword, learned whether Tiger Woods wears boxers or briefs (a thong, actually), how many teeth Phil Mickelson owns (912), and that the entrance to the world's largest dandruff mine lies in the committee room of the R&A in St. Andrews—and, in fact, that Saint Andrew himself only allowed golf to be played there because he thought it would eventually lead to ice hockey.

But I digress, and you've already read too far, indicating that you, like I, think way too much about this game already. Read on.

—David Feherty

INTRODUCTION

Golf is a funny game. It claims to be the most ancient of all those sporting activities soaking up television time, yet historians are having a tough time pegging its origins. Some speculate that Tiger Woods invented the game as we know it today, which is what people were saying about Greg Norman ten years earlier, or Tom Watson and Nancy Lopez a decade before that, or Jack Nicklaus a decade before that. Others insist Arnold Palmer pioneered the game, aligning its popularity with the emergence of televised golf and the Masters Tournament circa 1960. Still others will say, no, it was really Ben Hogan ten years earlier, or Byron Nelson ten years before that, or Bobby Jones ten years before that. On and on it goes, back through Walter Hagen, Francis Ouimet, Willie Anderson, Beatrix Hoyt, and Harry Vardon—and that gets us only as far back as the 1890s.

Various histories pinpoint the roots of the game as dating back more than five hundred years. Golf supposedly originated in either Holland or Scotland, depending on which day of the week you happen to be discussing the issue and whether your ancestors wore wooden shoes or kilts. Either way you slice (or hook) it, golf is a sport steeped in the years and rich in history and tradition. A lot of that history as well as some of those traditions are covered in *The Ultimate Golf Trivia Book*. There is something in here for all kinds of golfers and/or golf fans, regardless of generation, gender, nationality, handicap (or, yes, disability), shoe size, hat size, glove size, occupation, personality type, blood type, grip preference, taste in movies, taste in women or men, hair color, eye color, whether you are left-handed or right-handed, right-brained or left-brained, your ability to hit a one-iron, or whether or not you believe Bill Clinton has gotten away with too many mulligans in life.

Be assured that this handiwork isn't a mere regurgitation of names, dates, and places gleaned from a perfunctory study of media guides and one or two golf encyclopedias. Dozens of books and hundreds of golf periodicals were carefully reviewed for material, as were my own notes dating back over nearly twenty years of covering golf for various publications.

Please enjoy . . . and remember to keep your head down.

LOCAL RULES

The Ultimate Golf Trivia Book features an eighteen-hole (chapter) layout that is more than 1,000 Q&As in length and plays to a par of 72. There also are numerous rest stops and snack carts available in the form of top-ten lists, sidebars, and strange-but-true stories that offer a nice diversion, especially during those trying times when the foursome, or, Clifford Roberts forbid, the fivesome in front of you refuses to let you play through.

Singles can play any day of the week, including weekends, although golfers will have more fun going up against each other as match-play or stroke-play opponents. For those of you intent on keeping score, the following rules apply:

1. If playing by yourself and keeping score, you must pull from your golf bag a scorecard, towel, or some such device to use in covering the answers as you go down each page. Answers are given immediately after each question.
2. Twosomes are allowed and even encouraged.
3. As always, golf's honor system is in effect.
4. No mulligans.
5. Each player must have his or her own clubs and scoring pencil . . . and book (remember, the author gets paid only with royalties).
6. No speaking while the other player is taking a swing (or contemplating an answer).
7. Play the ball down and in your own fairway (no peeking at facing pages).
8. Ninety-degree rule in effect (i.e., no shortcuts, okay?).
9. Let faster book buyers through.
10. Soft spikes (that is, soft-lead pencils) only.

The
FRONT
nine

THE MAJORS

90 Questions
Par: 5

Q. Who are the only two golfers to have won a particular major tournament at least six times?

A. Harry Vardon (six British Opens) and Jack Nicklaus (six Masters Tournaments).

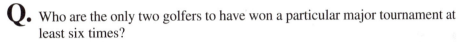

Q. The British Open trophy is actually what kind of object?

A. A claret jug.

Q. What two former San Jose State teammates met in a play-off at the 1992 U.S. Women's Open?

A. Patty Sheehan and Juli Inkster, and Sheehan won the play-off.

Q. What beneficiary of 1998 laser eye surgery and former U.S. Open champion finished a distant second behind Tiger Woods at the 1997 Masters?

A. Tom Kite.

Q. What golfer with a familiar-sounding last name bogied the last three holes of regulation in the 1979 Masters and then lost in a play-off?

A. Ed Sneed, who joined Tom Watson in losing a play-off to Fuzzy Zoeller.

Q. The 1967 U.S. Women's Open was won by what foreign-born amateur?

A. Catherine LaCoste, from France.

Q. In 1970 what future Ryder Cup captain became the first Brit in fifty years to win the U.S. Open?

A. Tony Jacklin.

———∞∞∞———

Q. The winner of the 1954 U.S. Open was what golfer whose left arm was six inches shorter than his right, the result of a childhood accident?

A. Ed Furgol.

———∞∞∞———

Q. Who is the youngest winner ever of a women's professional major?

A. Betty Hicks, who won the 1937 Western Open at age seventeen.

———∞∞∞———

Q. What teenager, other than Betty Hicks, also won a women's major in 1937?

A. Patty Berg, who won that year's Titleholders at the age of nineteen.

———∞∞∞———

Q. Who scored the first double eagle in men's U.S. Open play?

A. T. C. Chen, in 1985.

———∞∞∞———

Q. Who has been the only man to win three consecutive U.S. Opens?

A. Willie Anderson, in 1903, 1904, and 1905.

———∞∞∞———

Q. What sitting U.S. president was the first to present the U.S. Open trophy to the champion in the post-tournament ceremony?

A. Warren G. Harding, to Open winner James Barnes in 1921.

———∞∞∞———

Q. What twenty-year-old won the 1931 PGA Championship?

A. Tom Creavy.

Ten Great Golfers and the One Major Tournament Each Most Conspicuously Failed to Win (through 1998)

1. Sam Snead (U.S. Open)
2. Arnold Palmer (PGA Championship)
3. Nancy Lopez (U.S. Women's Open)
4. Patty Berg (LPGA Championship)
5. Tom Watson (PGA Championship)
6. Betsy Rawls (Titleholders)
7. Lee Trevino (Masters Tournament)
8. Byron Nelson (British Open)
9. Kathy Whitworth (U.S. Women's Open)
10. Raymond Floyd (British Open)

Q. Who was the last amateur before Jenny Chuasiriporn in 1998 to finish as high as second in a U.S. Women's Open?

A. Nancy Lopez, who tied for second as an amateur in 1975.

———∞———

Q. In which U.S. Open did brother beat brother in a play-off to win?

A. The 1910 Open at Philadelphia Cricket Club, where Alex Smith prevailed over his brother Macdonald Smith as well as John McDermott.

———∞———

Q. Ben Hogan's three-putt at the seventy-second hole in the 1946 Masters allowed what fellow three-putt finisher to win his only Masters title?

A. Herman Keiser.

———∞———

Q. Golfer Joe Kirkwood bogied three straight holes at the 1950 U.S. Open and missed a play-off by two strokes after being informed late in his round of what false but nerve-wracking information?

A. His father, Joe Kirkwood Sr., had been killed in an auto accident.

Q. By winning the PGA Championship in 1968 at the age of forty-eight, what golfer became the oldest man ever to win a major?

A. Julius Boros.

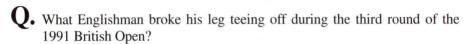

Q. What Englishman broke his leg teeing off during the third round of the 1991 British Open?

A. Richard Boxall.

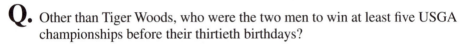

Q. Other than Tiger Woods, who were the two men to win at least five USGA championships before their thirtieth birthdays?

A. Bobby Jones and Jerome Travers.

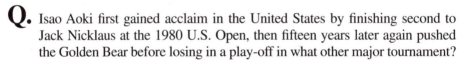

Q. Isao Aoki first gained acclaim in the United States by finishing second to Jack Nicklaus at the 1980 U.S. Open, then fifteen years later again pushed the Golden Bear before losing in a play-off in what other major tournament?

A. The 1995 Tradition.

Q. What is meant when it is said that Greg Norman won the 1986 "Saturday Slam"?

A. The Shark led or was tied for the lead in each of that year's four majors after three rounds (his only victory of the four, however, came in the British Open).

Q. The father/caddie of what amateur golfer competing in the 1998 U.S. Open was criticized for his seemingly overly exuberant behavior?

A. Matt Kuchar.

Q. What former fashion model's first-round 63 at the 1994 U.S. Women's Open set an Open low-scoring record?

A. Helen Alfredsson.

Lonely Shark

Even if Greg Norman were to chalk up a few more major-tournament victories before retiring to a life of leisure aboard his yacht *Aussi Rules,* he will forever be defined more by the majors he has lost than by those he has won (just two British Opens through 1998). One of Norman's distinctions is his having lost play-offs in each of the four majors (the 1984 U.S. Open, to Fuzzy Zoeller; the 1987 Masters, to Larry Mize; the 1989 British Open, to Mark Calcavecchia; and the 1993 PGA Championship, to Paul Azinger). But Norman isn't alone when it comes to touching all four bases of major-play-off failure. Craig Wood also pulled off a career "Near Slam," losing play-offs in the 1935 Masters (to Gene Sarazen), the 1939 U.S. Open (to Byron Nelson), the 1933 British Open (to Denny Shute), and the 1934 PGA Championship (to Paul Runyan).

Q. Who was the caddie on Ben Crenshaw's bag for both of Crenshaw's Masters victories, in 1984 and 1995?

A. Carl Jackson.

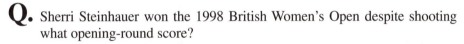

Q. Sherri Steinhauer won the 1998 British Women's Open despite shooting what opening-round score?

A. 81.

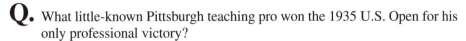

Q. What little-known Pittsburgh teaching pro won the 1935 U.S. Open for his only professional victory?

A. Sam Parks Jr.

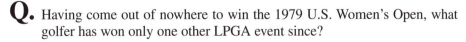

Q. Having come out of nowhere to win the 1979 U.S. Women's Open, what golfer has won only one other LPGA event since?

A. Jerilyn Britz.

Q. What was the first men's major tournament to go to a sudden-death play-off format?

A. The PGA Championship, in 1977, when Lanny Wadkins defeated Gene Littler in overtime.

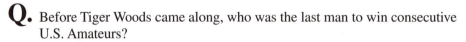

Q. Before Tiger Woods came along, who was the last man to win consecutive U.S. Amateurs?

A. Jay Sigel, in 1982 and 1983.

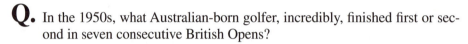

Q. In the 1950s, what Australian-born golfer, incredibly, finished first or second in seven consecutive British Opens?

A. Peter Thomson, from 1952 through 1958. Four of those were victories, and he won a fifth in 1965.

Q. Who was the last golfer to make it through both local and sectional qualifying en route to winning the U.S. Open?

A. Orville Moody, in 1969.

Q. Reigning Masters champion Sandy Lyle had what Scottish dish placed on the menu for the 1989 Masters Champions Dinner?

A. Haggis.

Q. Who was the first golfer to win the U.S. Senior Open?

A. Roberto De Vicenzo, in 1980.

Q. John Daly defeated what Italian golfer in a play-off to win the 1995 British Open?

A. Costantino Rocca.

Q. Of all the women's majors, the most notorious for its slow play is the U.S. Women's Open, as evidenced in 1991 at Fort Worth's Colonial Country Club when golfer Lori Garbacz did what while waiting to tee off in the middle of the round?

A. Ordered a pizza.

Q. What winner of four British Amateurs and two British Opens was the first Brit to win the U.S. Amateur?

A. Harold Hilton, in 1911.

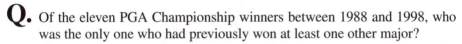

Q. Of the eleven PGA Championship winners between 1988 and 1998, who was the only one who had previously won at least one other major?

A. Nick Price, the 1994 PGA champ who had already won a British Open that summer and another PGA two years earlier.

Q. Who was the first American to win the U.S. Open?

A. John J. McDermott, in 1911.

Q. Who was the first American to win the British Open?

A. Walter Hagen, in 1922.

Q. What LPGA golfer was just two months short of her fortieth birthday when she made the 1994 du Maurier Classic her first major victory?

A. Martha Nause.

Q. In what year did Harry Vardon win his sixth British Open Championship, a record that still stands?

A. 1914.

Ten Men Whose First U.S. Tour Victory Came in a U.S. Open

1. Walter Hagen, 1914	6. Jack Nicklaus, 1962
2. Gene Sarazen, 1922	7. Lee Trevino, 1968
3. Sam Parks, 1935	8. Orville Moody, 1969
4. Julius Boros, 1952	9. Jerry Pate, 1976
5. Jack Fleck, 1955	10. Ernie Els, 1994

Q. After three-putting the seventy-second hole to lose the 1996 U.S. Open by one stroke, what golfer notched his first major victory a year later in the PGA Championship?

A. Davis Love III.

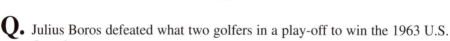

Q. What lumber salesman and amateur golfer rocked the world by nearly winning the 1954 Masters?

A. Billy Joe Patton.

Q. Julius Boros defeated what two golfers in a play-off to win the 1963 U.S. Open?

A. Arnold Palmer and Jacky Cupit.

Q. What former U.S. Open champion did Payne Stewart beat in a play-off to win the 1991 Open at Hazeltine?

A. Scott Simpson, who had won the 1987 Open at Olympic.

Harry Vardon won six British Open Championships between 1896 and 1914 and capped it all off with a U.S. Open title in 1900. Vardon was such a straight hitter, the legend goes, that during his prime he once went two years in competition without ever leaving the fairway.

(COURTESY OF THE LIBRARY OF CONGRESS)

Q. What runner-up to Nick Price at the 1994 British Open erred by failing to look at an updated leader board as he teed off eighteen in the final round?

A. Jesper Parnevik. Had he bothered to look, he would have noticed all he needed at the finishing hole was a par. Thinking he needed a birdie, Parnevik went awry and bogied to miss a play-off by one stroke.

───※───

Q. Horton Smith was the first winner of what major?

A. What is now known as the Masters Tournament, in 1934.

───※───

Q. What's the record for largest margin of victory in a U.S. Open?

A. Eleven strokes, by Willie Smith in 1899.

Q. St. Andrews has been the site of how many of Tom Watson's five British Open titles?

A. None.

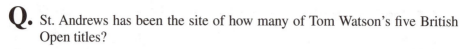

Q. The last PGA Championship to be contested in a match-play format had what winner?

A. Lionel Hebert, in 1957.

Q. Who was the last golfer before Tiger Woods to be reigning champion of three majors at once?

A. Jack Nicklaus, winner of the 1971 PGA Championship, 1972 Masters, and 1972 U.S. Open. Nicklaus also had the lead late in the 1972 British Open going for the Fiscal Year Grand Slam, but Lee Trevino won.

Q. Who was the first golfer to win both the U.S. Junior Amateur and the U.S. Open?

A. Johnny Miller, in 1964 and 1973, respectively.

Q. British legends Harry Vardon and Ted Ray were outdueled by what victorious twenty-year-old Yank at the 1913 U.S. Open?

A. Francis Ouimet.

Q. The 1985 U.S. Women's Open was the first professional victory for what golfer?

A. Kathy Baker (now Kathy Guadagnino).

Q. Ian Baker-Finch, the 1991 British Open champion, shot what first-round score in the 1997 British Open?

A. 92, and he immediately withdrew.

Ol' Mike Donald

Look up *journeyman* in the golfer's dictionary and see the photo of Mike Donald. Twenty years of toiling at the Tour produced the moniker of "Iron Mike" for Donald, whose penchant for grinding out more tournament appearances than most of his peers is legendary. Yet his only PGA Tour victory came in the 1989 Anheuser Busch Classic. Whether or not Donald ever again contends at a Greater Milwaukee Open or a Michelob Championship, he already can lay claim to his fifteen minutes of fame—twice, both in 1990. At Augusta that year Donald tied a Masters first-round record of 64 before cratering. Two months later at Medinah Country Club he took the great Hale Irwin down to the wire in a U.S. Open play-off, eventually losing when Irwin birdied the sudden-death nineteenth hole. Donald's longevity as a tour pro qualifies him as something more than a flash in the pan, and his 1990 play at the Masters and U.S. Open had him catching lightning in a bottle.

Mike Donald nearly pulled off the impossible in his 1990 U.S. Open play-off against Hale Irwin at Medinah. (©PHIL SHELDON)

Q. What three men aged forty years or older won two majors in the same calendar year?

A. Ben Hogan (1953), Jack Nicklaus (1980), and Mark O'Meara (1998).

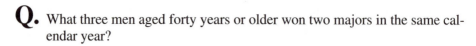

Q. One of John Travolta's most memorable movie characters had the same name as what former U.S. Open champion?

A. Tony Manero, winner of the 1936 Open at Baltusrol, has the same name as Travolta's stud dancer in *Saturday Night Fever*.

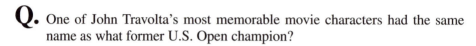

Q. Greg Norman's final-round meltdown at the 1996 Masters came on the anniversary date (April 14) of what two other notable tragedies?

A. Abraham Lincoln's assassination (1865) and the *Titanic*'s fatal collision with an iceberg (1912).

Q. What notoriously hot-tempered yet marvelously skilled golfer was caught on camera angrily flinging a golf club into the water at the 1960 U.S. Open?

A. Tommy Bolt.

Q. Hale Irwin's first senior major triumph came in what event?

A. The 1996 PGA Seniors' Championship.

Q. Amateur great Carol Semple Thompson has won national amateur championships in what three countries?

A. United States, Great Britain, and Mexico.

Q. Long after winner-to-be Fred Couples got a reprieve at the 1992 Masters when his Sunday tee shot at the par-three twelfth defied all odds by staying dry on the green's front embankment, Augusta officials confirmed what rumor regarding the greenkeeping crew?

A. The employee assigned to the twelfth hole had neglected to mow the embankment that day.

Q. Why did USGA officials hastily plant a twenty-five-foot spruce tree along the left side of the eighth tee at Inverness between rounds of the 1979 U.S. Open?

A. To block a clearing in the trees that had been exploited by golfer Lon Hinkle to shortcut the par-five hole. The spruce became known as Hinkle's Tree.

Q. Who was the first golfer to win five British Opens?

A. James Braid, after he had spotted Harry Vardon a 4-1 lead.

Q. After firing at the wrong flagstick, what golfer lost his lead and, ultimately, the tournament, at the 1970 British Open?

A. Lee Trevino.

Q. Jack Nicklaus's playing partner in the final round of his stirring victory at the 1986 Masters was what future Masters winner?

A. Sandy Lyle.

Q. Who was the first man to win four U.S. Opens?

A. Willie Anderson.

Q. Who was the first woman to win the U.S. Women's Open and British Women's Open in the same year?

A. Patty Sheehan, in 1992.

Q. A record five PGA Championships (later tied by Jack Nicklaus) was won by what dapper golfer?

A. Walter Hagen.

Q. The surprise first-round coleader in the 1977 U.S. Open at Southern Hills was what little-known Argentinean who had actually been playing the U.S. tour for two years?

A. Florentino Molina.

Q. What golfer was the first man to win the U.S. Open and U.S. Amateur in the same year?

A. Charles "Chick" Evans, in 1916.

Q. What turn-of-the-century British golf triumvirate won a total of sixteen British Opens among them?

A. Harry Vardon, James Braid, and John Henry Taylor.

Q. What dentist won two U.S. Opens and one Masters?

A. Dr. Cary Middlecoff.

Q. The first male lefty to go as low as a 65 in a single round at a major was what golfer?

A. Phil Mickelson, who shot a first-round 65 at the 1996 Masters.

Q. People said what four-time British Open champion's death at age twenty-four was the result of a broken heart?

A. Young Tom Morris, whose wife died in childbirth.

Golf did not begin with **Old Tom Morris** and **Young Tom Morris**, although it's easy to think of them as inventors of the sport. Morris Sr. won the British Open in 1861 (the second Open ever), 1862, 1864, and 1867. In stepped Tom Jr. to win in 1868, 1869, 1870, and 1872 (no championship was played in 1871).

(©PHIL SHELDON)

Q. After becoming the first man since Ben Hogan in 1950 and 1951 to win consecutive U.S. Opens, Curtis Strange opened his 1989 Open victory press conference with what appropriate three words?

A. "Move over, Ben."

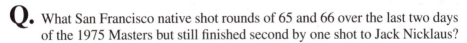

Q. What San Francisco native shot rounds of 65 and 66 over the last two days of the 1975 Masters but still finished second by one shot to Jack Nicklaus?

A. Johnny Miller.

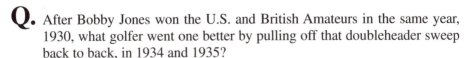

Q. After Bobby Jones won the U.S. and British Amateurs in the same year, 1930, what golfer went one better by pulling off that doubleheader sweep back to back, in 1934 and 1935?

A. Lawson Little.

Ten Amateurs with Top-Eight Finishes in Men's Majors Since 1960

1. Jack Nicklaus, second, 1960 U.S. Open
2. Guy Wostenholme, sixth, 1960 British Open
3. Joe Carr, eighth, 1960 British Open
4. Charlie Coe, second, 1961 Masters
5. Jack Nicklaus, tie for seventh, 1961 Masters
6. Jack Nicklaus, tie for fourth, 1961 U.S. Open
7. Billy Maxwell, tie for fifth, 1962 Masters
8. Johnny Miller, tie for eighth, 1966 U.S. Open
9. Jim Simons, tie for fifth, 1971 U.S. Open
10. Justin Rose, tie for fourth, 1998 British Open

Q. Who was the only man to play in both a Masters and baseball's World Series?

A. Sam Byrd, who played in the 1931 World Series for the New York Yankees and notched top-five finishes at the Masters in 1941 and 1942.

Q. What golfer apparently tied for a spot in a play-off at the 1940 U.S. Open, only to be disqualified for teeing off early in order to beat a brewing storm? (There was no USGA official at the first tee to stop him.)

A. Porky Oliver. The absent USGA official was eating lunch.

Q. In 1997 Nancy Lopez became the first golfer to shoot all four rounds in the 60s in a U.S. Women's Open only to lose by one shot to what diminutive European?

A. Alison Nicholas.

Q. Who was the first golfer ever to get to double figures in the red in a men's U.S. Open?

A. Gil Morgan, who made it all the way to thirteen under at the 1992 Open at Pebble Beach, before the breezes kicked up and swept Doc out of contention.

Q. Signing an incorrect scorecard disqualified what apparent winner of the 1957 U.S. Women's Open?

A. Jackie Pung.

Q. Other than Jack Nicklaus, who is the only man to win at least ten professional majors?

A. Walter Hagen, with eleven.

Q. After shooting a dreadful opening-round 80 in the 1985 Masters, what golfer rebounded to actually hold the back-nine lead in the final round before ultimately losing to Bernhard Langer?

A. Curtis Strange.

Q. Other than Willie Anderson, what three golfers have won at least four U.S. Opens?

A. Bobby Jones, Ben Hogan, and Jack Nicklaus.

Q. What American was in the lead at the halfway point of the 1977 British Open, which turned into an incredible thirty-six-hole duel between Jack Nicklaus and Tom Watson over the last two days?

A. Roger Maltbie.

Q. Who finished second to John Daly at the 1991 PGA Championship, three shots back?

A. Bruce Lietzke.

1

SCORECARD

90 Questions
Par: 5

Correct answers	Score	
87–90	Double eagle	2
80–86	Eagle	3
65–79	Birdie	4
45–64	Par	5
30–44	Bogey	6
15–29	Double Bogey	7
Less than 15	Triple Bogey	8

Your score _____

2 GOLF RULES, EQUIPMENT, AND ISSUES

70 Questions
Par: 4

Q. What was the old nickname for a two-wood?

A. Brassie.

———◦◦◦———

Q. A Callaway rep was caught in an apparent act of industrial espionage, when in 1998 he reportedly swiped a club from a golf bag belonging to what rival company?

A. Orlimar.

———◦◦◦———

Q. Alert television viewers watching the 1987 Andy Williams Open caught Craig Stadler in the act of unwittingly committing what rules violation that led to his disqualification?

A. The Walrus knelt on a towel in the rough while hitting a shot out from under a tree. Use of the towel violated the rule about building a stance.

———◦◦◦———

Q. What popular oversized club was named after a World War I cannon that had an unusually long range?

A. The Big Bertha.

———◦◦◦———

Q. What self-made millionaire businessman and PGA Tour veteran was installed as president of the controversial and fledgling Tournament Players Association, formed in 1998?

A. Danny Edwards.

Q. Muffin Spencer-Devlin rattled a few cages in 1996 when she became the first LPGA golfer to publicly admit to what?

A. Being a lesbian.

Q. The British scoring term *albatross* is synonymous with what American expression?

A. Double eagle.

Q. What company yanked its sponsorship of the Memorial Tournament reportedly after learning that Golden Bear International had hired a rival company to help Golden Bear with its initial public offering?

A. Dean Witter.

Q. How long do the Rules of Golf allow for a search before a missing ball must be declared lost?

A. Five minutes.

Q. What was the name of the club innovation Taylor Made devised in 1994 involving graphite and a shaft that gets progressively thicker the closer it gets to the handle before it thins out at the end?

A. Bubble shaft.

Q. Tiger Woods in 1997 breached an unwritten rule of peer protocol by refusing to autograph a ball left for him by what fellow pro golfer?

A. Billy Andrade, who was going to contribute the ball as one of a number of items to be auctioned off for Charities for Children.

Q. What prompted Tiger Woods to temporarily enact his no-autograph policy?

A. A request by fellow pro Ed Fiori to autograph some commemorative Masters flags he had collected—all thirty of them.

Strange but True

So, why do full-length golf courses traditionally have eighteen holes, and not twenty, or ten, or an even dozen? A bit of digging turns up a tale that takes us back to St. Andrews in 1858. During a discussion among the club's membership board, one of the members happened to point out that it takes exactly eighteen shots to polish off a fifth of Scotch. By limiting himself to only one shot per hole (shot of Scotch, that is), the Scot figured a round was finished when the rotgut ran out. So there you have it, the rationale behind eighteen holes, and the apparent forerunner of the popular golf 'n' guzzle format better known as Sniff 'n' Snort.

Q. His changing into shorts in a port-o-john during the middle of a 1983 U.S. Open round brought the wrath of the USGA down on what former U.S. Open runner-up?

A. Forrest Fezler, who finished second behind Hale Irwin in the 1974 U.S. Open.

Q. In 1998 what LPGA veteran became the first woman to sign an endorsement deal with NFL Properties to wear its line of apparel?

A. Danielle Ammaccapane.

Q. What American was videotaped apparently marking his ball incorrectly at the 1997 Trophée Lancôme and was still being pestered about it a year later while insisting on his innocence?

A. Mark O'Meara.

Q. The approach to the golf swing popularized and endorsed by golf savant Moe Norman is known by what name?

A. Natural Golf.

Q. While in a slump, what 1990s winner of a PGA Championship and Fort Worth native gave up his Callaway clubs to return to his preferred Hogans, even without a contract from the latter?

A. Mark Brooks, winner of the 1996 PGA.

───⊗∞⊗───

Q. To what media entity was Fuzzy Zoeller speaking when he made his infamous remarks at the 1997 Masters about Tiger Woods, fried chicken, and collard greens?

A. CNN.

───⊗∞⊗───

Q. The part of the golf club that connects the clubhead to the shaft is called what?

A. Hosel.

───⊗∞⊗───

Q. What golf industry mover and shaker has had CEO stints with the National Golf Foundation, the Hogan Company, Golfsmith, and the Pebble Beach Company?

A. David Hueber.

───⊗∞⊗───

Q. R&A is an abbreviation for what?

A. The Royal and Ancient Golf Club at St. Andrews.

───⊗∞⊗───

Q. What was the name of Paul Azinger's strange-looking putter he used to win the 1992 Tour Championship, featuring a shaft centered on a diamond-shaped clubhead? (Hint: It's the same name as a cheesy 1950s horror flick featuring James Arness, updated with a 1980s version starring Kurt Russell.)

A. The Thing.

───⊗∞⊗───

Q. What golfer lost a 1995 judgment to Cubic Balance by not playing its equipment as contracted?

A. David Frost.

Q. What was the term for the playing situation on the green when one golfer's ball obstructed the line of another's, requiring the latter to chip his or her ball over the one in front?

A. Stymie, which was outlawed in 1951 by the USGA and the R&A.

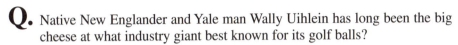

Q. Native New Englander and Yale man Wally Uihlein has long been the big cheese at what industry giant best known for its golf balls?

A. Titleist.

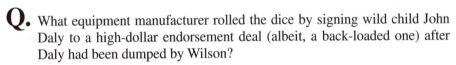

Q. What equipment manufacturer rolled the dice by signing wild child John Daly to a high-dollar endorsement deal (albeit, a back-loaded one) after Daly had been dumped by Wilson?

A. Callaway.

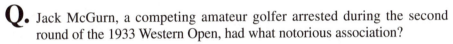

Q. Jack McGurn, a competing amateur golfer arrested during the second round of the 1933 Western Open, had what notorious association?

A. "Machine Gun Jack" was a hit man for Al Capone.

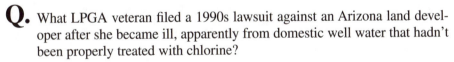

Q. What LPGA veteran filed a 1990s lawsuit against an Arizona land developer after she became ill, apparently from domestic well water that hadn't been properly treated with chlorine?

A. Caroline Keggi, who fell from thirty-first on the LPGA money list in 1992 to off the radar while battling a strange, lingering illness.

<hr />

Q. *Spoon* is another name for what club?

A. A three-wood.

<hr />

Q. What popular handicapping system, also called the Pinehurst system, is based on a single-round formula relative to a golfer's worst holes?

A. The Callaway system, named for its creator Lionel Callaway.

Q. In 1997 what PGA Tour player was arrested and charged with aggravated assault at a Duluth, Georgia, sports bar for allegedly pulling a knife on another man who had apparently hassled the golfer's female companion?

A. Frank Lickliter.

Q. The "main" PGA Merchandise Show is held annually in what city?

A. Orlando, Florida.

Q. What company known for its blue-light specials dumped Fuzzy Zoeller as a pitchman after the Fuzz made racist remarks about Tiger Woods at the 1997 Masters?

A. Kmart.

Q. Coburn Haskell, credited with the turn-of-the-century invention of the rubber-core golf ball, was an engineer for what Ohio-based company?

A. Goodrich.

Q. Golfer Tom Watson resigned his membership in the Kansas City Country Club in 1990 when the club, which had no Jewish members, rejected the application of what prominent Jewish businessman?

A. Henry Bloch, cofounder of H&R Block.

Q. What scoring system uses points instead of strokes at The International, played in Colorado?

A. Stableford.

Q. Who was the first African American to compete in a PGA Tour event?

A. Boxer Joe Louis, who made it through a qualifier into the field for the 1952 San Diego Open, although he then missed the cut.

Q. In 1994 Mac O'Grady charged that a number of the better golfers in the world were using what kind of medication to calm their nerves during tournament play?

A. Beta-blockers.

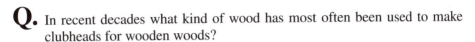

Q. In recent decades what kind of wood has most often been used to make clubheads for wooden woods?

A. Persimmon.

Q. Random-shooting victim and LPGA golfer Kim Williams signed an endorsement deal with what company soon after the shooting incident?

A. Bullet Golf.

Q. What's the time limit on waiting for a ball overhanging the cup to fall for it to count as a made putt?

A. Ten seconds.

Q. In 1997 what upstart putter manufacturer purchased Tommy Armour and Ram in consecutive months?

A. TearDrop.

Q. The R&A was, in effect, coerced into legalizing steel-shafted clubs in 1929 when what prominent golfer used them while playing the Old Course at St. Andrews?

A. The Prince of Wales (the future King Edward VIII).

Q. What is the proper name for those knee-length pants worn by golfers such as Payne Stewart, Patty Sheehan, Jim Ferree, and Rocky Thompson?

A. Plus fours.

Strange but True

A farmer in Germany certainly said a mouthful in 1994 when he filed a lawsuit against the owners of a neighboring golf club for what he claimed were the murders of thirty of his cows. He filed the suit after a veterinarian investigating the death of the bevos found a golf ball lodged in the throat of one of the recently deceased. Further investigation led to the discovery that, all told, the thirty cows had swallowed about two thousand golf balls that had apparently strayed from the grounds of the golf course into the farmer's cow pasture.

Q. What third-round coleader at the 1992 Million Dollar Challenge disqualified himself after learning that an on-course advertising sign he had moved to hit a shot had been declared an immovable object necessitating a (free) drop?

A. Nick Price.

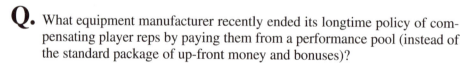

Q. What equipment manufacturer recently ended its longtime policy of compensating player reps by paying them from a performance pool (instead of the standard package of up-front money and bonuses)?

A. Karsten Manufacturing, now officially known as Ping.

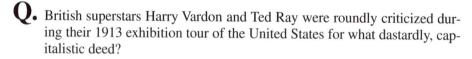

Q. British superstars Harry Vardon and Ted Ray were roundly criticized during their 1913 exhibition tour of the United States for what dastardly, capitalistic deed?

A. They charged the astronomical sum of $350 per appearance.

Q. In modern parlance what is a mashie-niblick?

A. A seven-iron.

Q. What African American, a former USGA executive committeeman, was later fired as general counsel to the ETW Corporation by Earl and Tiger Woods?

A. John Merchant.

———⊗⊗⊗———

Q. What material used in the manufacture of golf balls was banned for such use by the U.S. government during World War II?

A. Rubber.

———⊗⊗⊗———

Q. What American golfer explained his decision to skip the British Open one year by referring to St. Andrews as "the most piece of mess I've ever seen"?

A. Scott Hoch.

———⊗⊗⊗———

Q. The Hogan Company in the late eighties produced what highly acclaimed signature brand of forged-cavity-backed irons, which ultimately failed to fulfill their promise when the company was unable to meet popular demand in a timely manner?

A. The Edge.

———⊗⊗⊗———

Q. The mechanical device used by the USGA to simulate golf swings in the testing of equipment goes by what nickname?

A. Iron Byron.

———⊗⊗⊗———

Q. What parent company of Foot-Joy and Titleist completed its triumvirate by acquiring Cobra in 1996?

A. American Brands.

———⊗⊗⊗———

Q. The lawsuit brought by Karsten Manufacturing against the PGA Tour in the early 1990s concerned the tour's ban of what kind of iron clubfaces?

A. Square (U) grooves.

Litigious Links:
Ten Cases Involving Golf and/or Golfers in Which Lawyers Called the Shots

1. The square-grooves case that pitted Karsten Solheim against the PGA Tour
2. Casey Martin vs. the PGA Tour over the use of a golf cart in Tour-sanctioned competition
3. Mac O'Grady against the PGA Tour
4. The lawsuit brought by the guardians of two local boys shot by a security guard when they trespassed on the grounds of Augusta National Golf Club
5. A caddie's lawsuit against actor Michael Douglas, in which Douglas was accused of hitting the caddie in the groin with an errant shot and then calling the caddie a racial slur as he stuffed some money in the caddie's pocket
6. Harry Toscano vs. the Senior PGA Tour over the Tour's criteria for players' exemptions
7. Tiger Woods's suing the Franklin Mint for cutting a commemorative (but unauthorized) Masters Tournament medal featuring Woods
8. The case of the young man from Vancouver arrested for stealing private property after donning a wetsuit and diving into a lake at a golf course to retrieve golf balls
9. The California case of Mary Ann Warfield, awarded her husband's country-club membership in their divorce settlement, only to be denied access by the club because she was a woman
10. The case of counterfeiting that featured Callaway Golf's raid of a factory in Taiwan that had been manufacturing copycat Callaway equipment

Q. What son of a former heavyweight boxing champ made it to the top of his company, taking over as president and CEO of Izzo Systems in 1996?

A. Joe Louis Barrow Jr.

━━━━━∞∞∞━━━━━

Q. What USGA scoring-related mechanism was put into effect in 1912?

A. A national handicap system.

Strange but True

Golf-ball manufacturers at the turn of the twentieth century engaged in a hotly contested race to see who would be the first to discover the ideal core material to replace rubber and thus enhance the "liveliness" of ball flight. Among the materials experimented with in those early days were mercury, cork, lead, and—all Chevy "Fletch" Chase kidding aside—even ball bearings.

Q. Jim Stahl, 1995 Senior Amateur champ, ran into what human buzz saw of rudeness (a playing partner) while trying to compete in the 1996 Senior Open?

A. Playing partner Tom Weiskopf, who made it abundantly clear he didn't appreciate, among other things, Stahl's inadvertently teeing off out of turn on one hole or marking his ball with a quarter.

Q. What is the diameter of a golf hole?

A. Four and a quarter inches.

Q. In 1954 the USGA gave what ground-level gift to President Eisenhower?

A. A putting green on the south lawn of the White House.

Q. What legendary golfer is credited with inventing the sand wedge?

A. Gene Sarazen, in 1930.

Q. Where does the word *bogey* come from?

A. The British literary character Colonel Bogey, who was described as steady, not brilliant.

Ely Callaway emerged in the 1990s as perhaps the second-most recognizable equipment-manufacturing CEO in America. Here he is seen taking in the action at the 1998 U.S. Open at Olympic.

(©PHIL SHELDON)

Q. What well-known tennis player, also an avid golfer, was buried with his five-iron following his untimely death in 1994?

A. Vitas Gerulaitis.

Q. During a sales slump in 1998, Callaway Golf chairman Ely Callaway fired what longtime executive and demoted himself into the presidency of the company?

A. Don Dye.

Q. What is the golf term referring to a shot played over without penalty that is synonymous with President Bill Clinton?

A. Mulligan.

———✇———

Q. What's the penalty for hitting a ball out of bounds?

A. Stroke plus distance (*not* two strokes, as commonly used).

———✇———

Q. What kind of devices that improve blood flow have pro golfers been wearing on a variety of body locations in recent years to relieve their aches and pains?

A. Magnets.

———✇———

Q. What former LPGA vice president joined Arnold Palmer Golf in 1998 as president and CEO?

A. Cindy Davis.

———✇———

Q. Secret Service agents were dispatched by the White House to Congressional for the 1997 U.S. Open to learn the identity of the company that had manufactured a mystery titanium driver being used by what golfer?

A. Justin Leonard.

———✇———

Q. Former U.S. Amateur champion Nathaniel Crosby, Bing's boy, resigned as president of what company in 1998 to accept a position as executive vice president with Orlimar Golf Company?

A. Nicklaus Golf.

2

SCORECARD

70 Questions
Par: 4

Correct answers	Score	
68–70	Eagle	2
50–67	Birdie	3
35–49	Par	4
25–34	Bogey	5
10–24	Double Bogey	6
Less than 10	Triple Bogey	7

Your score _____

THE SIXTIES

40 Questions
Par: 3

Q. Who became the youngest winner of a PGA Tour event in more than thirty years by capturing the 1963 St. Petersburg Open?

A. Raymond Floyd, at the age of twenty years, six months, thirteen days.

━━━━ ⊙⊗⊗⊙ ━━━━

Q. While playing for what Big Ten School did Jack Nicklaus win his lone NCAA individual golf title, in 1961?

A. Ohio State.

━━━━ ⊙⊗⊗⊙ ━━━━

Q. What blatantly racist policy was finally stricken from the PGA's constitution in 1961?

A. The Caucasians-only clause.

━━━━ ⊙⊗⊗⊙ ━━━━

Q. A six-putt green in the 1967 Canadian Open jumped up and bit what former Masters winner known as a terrific putter...normally?

A. Doug Ford.

━━━━ ⊙⊗⊗⊙ ━━━━

Q. In 1969 what future LPGA golfer won the New Mexico women's amateur at age twelve?

A. Nancy Lopez.

Tony Lema embraces the claret jug that is his by virtue of winning the 1964 British Open Championship. A plane crash in 1966 took Lema's life just when he was hitting his stride. Not only was he the life of the party, Lema was a wonderful golfer who had already won fourteen events when he died. He was probably good for another dozen or so had his career been a full one. His life sure was. (SIDNEY HARRIS PHOTO, ©PHIL SHELDON)

Q. What halfway leader at the 1966 Pensacola Open got so caught up signing autographs at the end of his round that he forgot to sign his scorecard and was subsequently disqualified?

A. Doug Sanders.

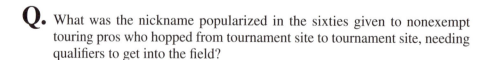

Q. What was the nickname popularized in the sixties given to nonexempt touring pros who hopped from tournament site to tournament site, needing qualifiers to get into the field?

A. Rabbits.

Q. Tony Lema's last victory before his death in a 1966 plane crash came in what tournament?

A. The 1966 Oklahoma City Open.

Q. At what golf course did Mickey Wright become the first LPGA golfer to go as low as 62 in an official event?

A. Hogan Park, in Midland, Texas, site of the 1964 Tall City Open.

Q. A last-minute withdrawal from the 1966 U.S. Open at Olympic opened a spot in the field for a young Johnny Miller, canceling his plans to do what that week?

A. Caddie in the Open.

Q. African-American Charlie Sifford's first official PGA Tour victory came in what event?

A. The 1967 Greater Hartford Open.

Q. What notoriety-challenged golfer whose last name rhymes with the word *who* briefly stunned the sports world by firing a 69 in the first round of the 1961 U.S. Open, giving him the only sub-par round of the day?

A. Bob Brue.

Q. Who finished second to Jack Nicklaus for most majors won during the 1960s?

A. Arnold Palmer, with six to Jack's seven.

Q. What players' organization broke away from the PGA in 1968, eventually leading to the formation of the PGA Tour?

A. The Association of Professional Golfers (APG).

A Slow Month

When people said that Don January really took his time at the 1963 Phoenix Open, they weren't kidding. In those days, eons before the PGA Tour finally put a stopwatch to slow players, January nearly turned into February and March while the lanky Texan lingered seven minutes at the last hole waiting for his lip-hugging putt to drop. It never did, and neither did the four-footer that an iced-out Gary Player missed moments later. Had Player made the putt, he would have forced a play-off with Arnold Palmer, who instead won outright. Between clenched teeth, Player later said, "January didn't have a right to wait that long for the putt to drop. It wasn't going to drop ever, not without hitting it."

Q. Ken Venturi's last PGA Tour victory came in what event?

A. The 1966 Lucky International.

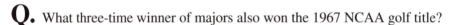

Q. What three-time winner of majors also won the 1967 NCAA golf title?

A. Hale Irwin, who also played football at the University of Colorado.

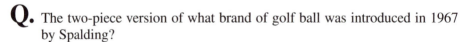

Q. The two-piece version of what brand of golf ball was introduced in 1967 by Spalding?

A. Top-Flite.

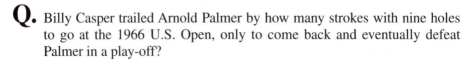

Q. Who won the most women's majors during the 1960s?

A. Mickey Wright, with ten.

Q. Billy Casper trailed Arnold Palmer by how many strokes with nine holes to go at the 1966 U.S. Open, only to come back and eventually defeat Palmer in a play-off?

A. Seven.

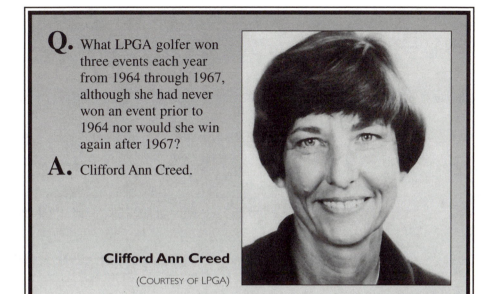

Q. What LPGA golfer won three events each year from 1964 through 1967, although she had never won an event prior to 1964 nor would she win again after 1967?

A. Clifford Ann Creed.

Clifford Ann Creed

(COURTESY OF LPGA)

Q. What twenty-three-year-old amateur grabbed the first-round lead at the 1967 U.S. Open by firing a 67 at Baltusrol and was still in the lead after three rounds, only to falter on Sunday with an 80?

A. Marty Fleckman.

Q. What ten-year-old made her LPGA debut in 1967?

A. Beverly Klass.

Q. Before New Zealander Bob Charles knocked in a short putt at the seventy-second hole of the 1963 British Open, which he later won in a play-off, his playing partner Phil Rodgers performed what prank that failed to amuse Charles?

A. Rodgers, the Jack Nicklaus look-alike who failed to fulfill his promise as a Nicklaus play-alike, took off his cap after holing out and covered the hole with it.

Q. Bob Murphy won the 1965 U.S. Amateur by one shot over what golfer who was assessed a four-stroke penalty for carrying too many clubs, before the latter went on to win both the U.S. and British Amateurs in 1967?

A. Bob Dickson.

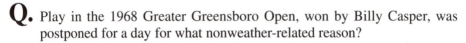

Q. Play in the 1968 Greater Greensboro Open, won by Billy Casper, was postponed for a day for what nonweather-related reason?

A. A national day of mourning for slain civil rights leader Dr. Martin Luther King Jr.

Q. What did tournament officials do in 1965 to the last two greens at Bellerive to make them look better on TV for the first color telecast of a U.S. Open?

A. Spray-painted them—green, of course.

Q. What golfer and future PGA Tour winner once went microscopic with a double nickel, shooting an unheard-of 55 in the 1962 Premier Invitational in Longview, Texas?

A. Homero Blancas.

Q. Although Sam Snead popularized the technique, Bob Duden is credited with inventing what putting stroke banned by the USGA in 1966?

A. The croquet-style of putting, in which the golfer faces the hole in his stance and putts from between his legs. Snead later switched to a "side-saddle" mode of putting.

Q. What was the first women's tournament to get live television coverage?

A. The 1963 U.S. Women's Open (final round only).

Ten Notables Whose Only Major Victory Came in the 1960s (Each Year Represented)

1. Jay Hebert, 1960 PGA Championship
2. Gene Littler, 1961 U.S. Open
3. Judy Kimball, 1962 LPGA Championship
4. Bob Charles, 1963 British Open
5. Ken Venturi, 1964 U.S. Open
6. Dave Marr, 1965 PGA Championship
7. Al Geiberger, 1966 PGA Championship
8. Gay Brewer, 1967 Masters
9. Sandra Post, 1968 LPGA Championship
10. George Archer, 1969 Masters

Q. Who were the only three Americans to win the British Open during the 1960s?

A. Arnold Palmer (1961 and 1962), Tony Lema (1964), and Jack Nicklaus (1966).

Q. Who was the 1960 PGA Championship winner whose brother had won the same event three years earlier?

A. Jay Hebert, whose brother Lionel won the PGA in 1957.

Q. When Donna Caponi won her first pro victory in the 1969 U.S. Women's Open, what delayed her final-hole birdie for fifteen minutes?

A. A thunderstorm.

Q. Who won the last men's major conducted in the 1960s?

A. Raymond Floyd, in the 1969 PGA Championship.

Q. Of the dozens of Young Turks coming onto the golf scene who have been dubbed "the next Jack Nicklaus," who arguably was the original member of that thankless fraternity?

A. Tom Weiskopf, two years Nicklaus's junior, a teammate of the Golden Bear's at Ohio State in 1960.

Q. What golfer won thirteen of the thirty LPGA events she entered in 1963?

A. Mickey Wright, who won seventy-nine tournaments during a twelve-year stretch in the fifties and sixties.

Q. After losing a play-off at the 1961 PGA Championship, what golfer finally won the event six years later, in 1967, also in a play-off?

A. Don January, who lost a 1961 play-off to Jerry Barber, then defeated Don Massengale in 1967.

Q. By what margin did Arnold Palmer win the 1962 British Open at Royal Troon?

A. Six strokes, over Kel Nagle.

Q. What future U.S. Open runner-up was the medalist in the PGA Tour's first Q-School finals, held in 1965?

A. John Schlee, who went on to finish second to Johnny Miller in the 1973 U.S. Open.

Q. Who was the first man to earn a winner's check as big as $50,000 in a PGA Tour event?

A. Jack Nicklaus, winner of the 1967 Westchester Classic.

Q. In 1969 Kathy Whitworth won four of the first five LPGA events, yet finished second to whom in most tournaments won that year?

A. Carol Mann, who totaled eight victories to Whitworth's seven.

3

SCORECARD

40 Questions
Par: 3

Correct answers	Score	
40	Ace	1
30–39	Birdie	2
20–29	Par	3
10–19	Bogey	4
Less than 10	Double Bogey	5

Your score _____

4
COURSES AND DESIGNERS

60 Questions
Par: 4

Q. At what country club and occasional U.S. Open site can one find the "church pews" (bunkers)?

A. Oakmont.

———∞∞———

Q. What seaside course, opened in 1919, was designed by Jack Neville, a five-time California state amateur champion?

A. Pebble Beach.

———∞∞———

Q. Before being removed from the British Open's rotation in the 1920s, what course hosted the first twelve Opens and twenty-four in all?

A. Prestwick.

———∞∞———

Q. In 1986 Greg Norman won the Kemper Open the last time it was played at what future site of the 1997 U.S. Open?

A. Congressional.

———∞∞———

Q. What is the 2002 U.S. Open site that underwent a $2.7 million facelift in 1998?

A. Bethpage Black.

———∞∞———

Q. Escalators have been installed on many courses in what predominantly hilly Far Eastern country to help golfers move from hole to hole?

A. Japan.

Ten Golf Courses with Names That Suggest Maybe It's Best Y'all Stay Away

Bloody Point Club, Daufuskie Island, South Carolina

Broken Woods Golf and Racquet Club, Coral Springs, Florida

Bull Valley Golf Club, Woodstock, Illinois

Double Dam Golf Club, Claysville, Pennsylvania

Dub's Dread Golf Club, Lawrence, Kansas

Nutcracker Golf Club, Granbury, Texas

Potholes Golf and Camping, Othello, Washington

Predator Ridge Golf Resort, Vernon, British Columbia

Sarah Shank Golf Course, Indianapolis, Indiana

Sunken Meadow State Park Golf Club, Kings Park, New York

(SOURCE: *Golf Digest*)

Q. The original site of the Legends of Golf Tournament was what Austin, Texas, venue?

A. Onion Creek.

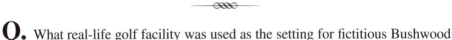

Q. What real-life golf facility was used as the setting for fictitious Bushwood Country Club in the flick *Caddyshack*?

A. Rolling Hills Country Club, in Davie, Florida.

Q. What longtime New England home for a PGA Tour event bid adieu to the Tour after Steve Pate won the tour's last official event there, the 1998 CVS Charity Classic?

A. Pleasant Valley Country Club, in Sutton, Massachusetts.

Q. Billionaire Howard Hughes purchased what Nevada golf course for $2.25 million in 1969?

A. Paradise Valley, site in those days of the Sahara Invitational.

The Pacific Ocean bordering Pebble Beach Golf Links in California offers a nice backdrop to **Tom Kite** as he plays his way to victory in the 1992 U.S. Open. (©PHIL SHELDON)

Q. The ashes of 1965 PGA Championship winner and veteran TV golf commentator Dave Marr were spread over what golf course?

A. Houston Memorial Park, where Marr learned the game while growing up.

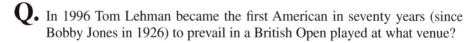

Q. What Atlantic Coast course and PGA Tour stop is distinguished by its red-and-white lighthouse?

A. Harbour Town.

Q. In 1996 Tom Lehman became the first American in seventy years (since Bobby Jones in 1926) to prevail in a British Open played at what venue?

A. Royal Lytham and St. Anne's.

Q. Which is the only course in Ireland that has hosted a British Open Championship?

A. Royal Portrush, in 1951.

Q. What prominent designer first gained notoriety in 1969 by working with Jack Nicklaus in laying out Harbour Town Golf Links?

A. Pete Dye.

Q. Low-lying seaside terrain and numerous sand dunes characterize what general category of golf courses?

A. Links.

Q. Where was the World Series of Golf played until it was modified into a different event in 1999?

A. Firestone Country Club, in Akron, Ohio.

Q. British architect Desmond Muirhead showed his Old World upbringing by inserting a par-five hole at Covington Plantation near Atlanta shaped like what?

A. A woman's body.

Q. Tony Jacklin and Payne Stewart won U.S. Opens at what Minnesota venue, which golfer Dave Hill once described as a cow pasture?

A. Hazeltine.

Q. On what Donald Ross-designed course did Curtis Strange win his second consecutive U.S. Open, in 1989?

A. Oak Hill.

Strange but True

Carnoustie, in Scotland, host site to six British Open Championships counting 1999, is like many venerated old golf courses in that it has a carefully chosen nickname for each of its eighteen holes. One of the more peculiar of Carnoustie's hole appellations is the tenth hole, otherwise known as South America. Now, we all know that Carnoustie bears little resemblance to Brazilian rain forests, but there is a good reason for the hole's moniker, and it's buried in club lore. It seems long ago there was a young lad of a caddie who one night had had a bit too many wee nips at the nineteenth hole. Far removed from a state of sobriety, the young man declared that night that he was going to head out for South America in search of fame and fortune. He never made it. In fact, he didn't even make it off the club's premises, awakening the next morning lying next to the tenth hole. It seems his short stopover had turned into a long hangover.

Q. What links golf club in Ireland, officially formed in 1906, includes an "Emerald Isle desert" at its eighteenth hole?

A. Ballybunion.

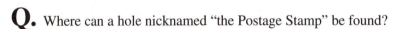

Q. Where can a hole nicknamed "the Postage Stamp" be found?

A. At Scotland's Royal Troon—the 128-yard eighth hole.

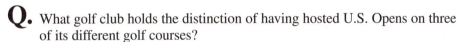

Q. What golf club holds the distinction of having hosted U.S. Opens on three of its different golf courses?

A. Baltusrol.

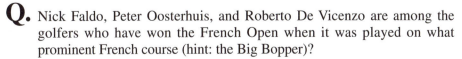

Q. Nick Faldo, Peter Oosterhuis, and Roberto De Vicenzo are among the golfers who have won the French Open when it was played on what prominent French course (hint: the Big Bopper)?

A. Golf de Chantilly.

Q. Which member of golf's original "Great Triumvirate" laid out many of the holes at Gleneagles in Scotland?

A. James Braid.

Q. Where can one find "Devlin's Billabong"?

A. Fronting the eighteenth green at Torrey Pines, where golfer Bruce Devlin's title hopes once went to a watery grave.

Q. What frequent U.S. Open course on the East Coast features bunkers shaped out of ancient Native American burial grounds?

A. Shinnecock Hills.

Q. It took Fred Couples two tries before his application for membership was accepted in 1998 at what prestigious West Coast club?

A. Los Angeles Country Club.

Q. Who partnered with golfer/designer Tom Weiskopf in the course-design business for nine years before they parted ways in 1994?

A. Jay Morrish.

Q. What four-time winner of the U.S. Open won his first of the four at L.A.'s Riviera in 1948?

A. Ben Hogan.

Q. On what English course did Seve Ballesteros win his first British Open title, in 1979?

A. Royal Lytham and St. Anne's.

The Swilcan Bridge gracing the eighteenth fairway of the Old Course at St. Andrews has seen great golfers come and go for more than a century. This group of nineteenth-century golfers and caddies includes "Old" Tom Morris (far left, on bridge), playing the hole backwards. (©PHIL SHELDON)

Q. The first time the Ryder Cup Matches were contested in Spain (1997), what was the host site?

A. Valderrama.

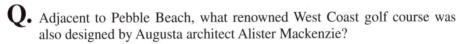

Q. Adjacent to Pebble Beach, what renowned West Coast golf course was also designed by Augusta architect Alister Mackenzie?

A. Cypress Point.

Q. What former U.S. Open golf course was so impressive that it was later converted into a business park?

A. Englewood Golf Club in New Jersey, which hosted the 1909 Open.

Q. How many golf courses comprise Pinehurst in North Carolina?

A. Eight.

Ten Favorite Names for U.S. Golf Courses
(from the National Golf Foundation, as of 1998)

1. Riverside, used 46 times
2. Lakeview, 40
3. Rolling Hills, 38
4. Hillcrest, 37
5. Lakeside, 37
6. Arrowhead, 33
7. Lakewood, 28
8. Twin Lakes, 27
9. Hidden Valley, 26
10. Meadowbrook, 26

(LIST REPRINTED IN *Golf World*)

Q. What frequent U.S. Open site is unofficially known as one of the birthplaces of women's golf?

A. Shinnecock Hills, which opened in 1891 with a coed membership of forty-four.

Q. On what course did Jack Nicklaus win his first of three British Open titles?

A. Muirfield, in 1966.

Q. After the copycat course Tour 18 was opened near Houston in 1993, offering replicas of eighteen of the world's most notable holes, what was the first copied course to come calling with a trademark-infringement lawsuit?

A. Pebble Beach.

Q. What midwestern U.S. Open venue was built in the 1920s as a private club for the Shriners?

A. Medinah.

Q. On what course did Johnny Miller capture his only British Open victory?

A. Royal Birkdale, in 1976.

Golf-course designer **Donald Ross** left a legacy of wondrous layouts which include Oakland Hills and Pinehurst No. 2.

(COURTESY OF LIBRARY OF CONGRESS)

Q. Which American venue ended the twentieth century as host site for the most men's major tournaments?

A. Augusta National, of course.

Q. In the 1970s Jack Nicklaus designed what Ontario course to be the permanent site of the Canadian Open?

A. Glen Abbey.

Q. What Down Under tournament layout is actually a composite of twelve holes from its West course, designed by Alister Mackenzie, and six holes from the newer East layout, designed by Mackenzie protégé Alex Russell?

A. Royal Melbourne, in Australia.

Q. What American venue hosted three men's major championships between 1972 and 1982?

A. Pebble Beach: U.S. Opens in 1972 and 1982; PGA Championship in 1977.

Q. The stone structure crossing a stream onto the eighteenth fairway at St. Andrews's Old Course goes by what name?

A. Swilcan Bridge.

Q. Where did Ben Hogan courageously win the 1950 U.S. Open, a little more than a year after he was almost crippled in an auto accident?

A. Merion.

Q. What designer supervised the construction of Baltusrol's two new eighteen-hole layouts soon after amateur Jerome Travers won the 1915 U.S. Open there?

A. A. W. Tillinghast.

Q. What golf course has been called "the Monster" since 1951 when Ben Hogan won his second consecutive U.S. Open title there?

A. Oakland Hills, in Michigan.

Q. In what New York community is Winged Foot located?

A. Mamaroneck.

Q. What two well-known golf venues are both nicknamed "Hogan's Alley"?

A. Los Angeles's Riviera and Fort Worth's Colonial.

Ten Great Disabled-Accessible Golf Courses

According to *We* magazine, a publication devoted to the disabled, the following ten North American golf facilities offer the best combination of quality golf course with outstanding accessibility for disabled golfers:

1. The Phoenician, Scottsdale, Arizona
2. Grenelefe Golf Resort, Haines City, Florida
3. Fox Hollow Resort, Lakewood, Colorado
4. The Orchid of Mauna Lani, Hawaii
5. Scottsdale Country Club, Scottsdale, Arizona
6. Walt Disney World–Lake Buena Vista Course, Orlando, Florida
7. Sheraton El Conquistador Resort and Country Club, Tucson, Arizona
8. Bethpage State Park, Farmingdale, New York
9. Greenbriar Country Club, Saskatoon, Saskatchewan
10. Grand Harbor, Vero Beach, Florida

(LIST REPRINTED IN *Golf World*)

Q. What Florida PGA Tour stop is best known for its island green at the seventeenth hole?

A. TPC at Sawgrass, host site of the Players Championship.

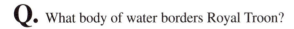

Q. What body of water borders Royal Troon?

A. The Firth of Clyde.

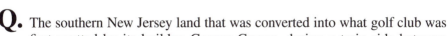

Q. The southern New Jersey land that was converted into what golf club was first spotted by its builder, George Crump, during a train ride between Philadelphia and Atlantic City?

A. Pine Valley.

Strange but True

Two of golf's greatest names are Bobby Jones and Robert Trent Jones, who weren't related, even though both of their names are Robert T. Jones. The former's middle name was Tyre. Bobby Jones was the greatest amateur golfer of the twentieth century and co-founder of perhaps the greatest golf course built in the twentieth century, Augusta National. Robert Trent Jones knew a thing or two about course design himself, having applied his architectural handiwork to such classics as Baltusrol and Spyglass Hill. The latter Jones's golf-design credo was "hard par, easy bogey," which is pertinent to the vision Bobby Jones had in helping to lay out Augusta. In fact, Robert Trent Jones had a hand in helping the other R. T. Jones with some re-design work at Augusta, including the sixteenth hole, in the late 1940s. Are you sure these two guys weren't related?

Q. North Carolina's Pinehurst has long been the regular host site of what prominent amateur tournament?

A. The North and South Championship.

Q. What Caribbean course designed by Pete Dye has a Spanish name that suggests a bite worse than its bark?

A. Casa de Campo, in the Dominican Republic. It translates into "Teeth of the Dog Course."

Q. What 1952 U.S. Open site in Dallas had a street running through it?

A. Northwood Country Club.

Q. Designer Donald Ross allegedly based many of his U.S. designs, such as Oak Hill, on what very old course in northeastern Scotland that dates back to 1616?

A. Royal Dornoch.

Q. The "Blue Monster" is the moniker given to what Florida golf course?

A. Doral's Blue Course, in Miami.

Q. The Falsterbo GolfKlubb links course, occupying a peninsula bordered on one side by the Baltic Sea, can be found in what country?

A. Sweden.

Q. What golfing great teamed up with what acting legend to build a golf course in France?

A. Jack Nicklaus and Sean Connery.

4

SCORECARD

60 Questions
Par: 4

Correct answers	Score	
58–60	Eagle	2
45–57	Birdie	3
30–44	Par	4
20–29	Bogey	5
10–19	Double Bogey	6
Less than 10	Triple Bogey	7

Your score _____

5 JONES, HAGEN, AND SARAZEN

40 Questions
Par: 3

Q. How old was Bobby Jones when he retired from full-time competitive golf?

A. Twenty-eight, in 1930.

———∞∞∞———

Q. What was Gene Sarazen's real name?

A. Eugenio Saraceni.

———∞∞∞———

Q. Who is the only man other than Bobby Jones named a Burgess of the Borough by the folks at St. Andrews?

A. Benjamin Franklin.

———∞∞∞———

Q. Jones was born in 1902 on what day celebrated annually?

A. St. Patrick's Day.

———∞∞∞———

Q. In what New York town did Walter Hagen grow up?

A. Rochester.

———∞∞∞———

Q. How old was Gene Sarazen when he won the U.S. Open for the first time, in 1922?

A. Twenty.

Newly retired **Bobby Jones** enjoys life as a camera-toting spectator at the 1931 Ryder Cup Matches in Columbus, Ohio.

(©PHIL SHELDON)

Q. What was Bobby Jones's occupation away from the golf course?

A. Attorney.

Q. On what hole at Augusta National is Sarazen's Bridge located?

A. The fifteenth, where he scored his double eagle en route to winning the 1935 Masters.

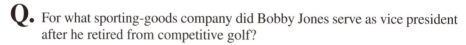

Q. For what sporting-goods company did Bobby Jones serve as vice president after he retired from competitive golf?

A. Spalding.

Q. How did Gene Sarazen, already the winner of a U.S. Open and a PGA Championship, fare in his first crack at the British Open, in 1923?

A. He failed to qualify.

Q. What Scotsman was Bobby Jones's best-known teacher of the game?

A. Stewart Maiden.

Q. How big a winner's check did Gene Sarazen receive for winning the 1935 Masters?

A. Fifteen hundred dollars.

Q. Who bestowed the nickname "Emperor Jones" on Bobby Jones?

A. Eugene O'Neill, author of a play with that title.

Q. The PGA Tour's 1998 Tour Championship was played at what Atlanta venue best known as Jones's home course (at least before Augusta National came along)?

A. East Lake.

Q. Walter Hagen once uttered the memorable phrase in which he said he never intended to become a *what*, only to live like one?

A. Millionaire.

Q. What was the series name of the first group of instructional film shorts that Bobby Jones made?

A. *How I Play Golf*, which included twelve films.

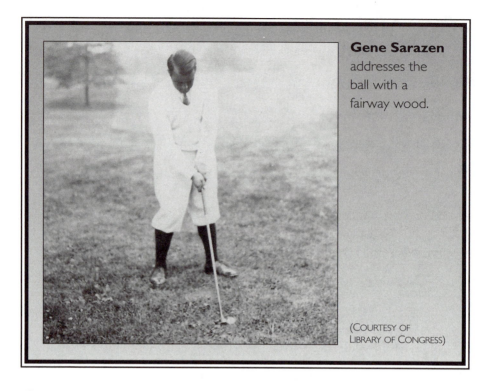

Gene Sarazen addresses the ball with a fairway wood.

(COURTESY OF LIBRARY OF CONGRESS)

Q. At what future U.S. Open site did Walter Hagen serve as a club professional in his early days as a pro?

A. Oakland Hills, near Detroit.

Q. What four events comprised the Grand Slam that Bobby Jones won in 1930?

A. U.S. Open, U.S. Amateur, British Open, and British Amateur.

Q. With what major studio did Jones produce his instructional films?

A. Warner Brothers.

Q. Where was the first of Walter Hagen's two U.S. Open victories?

A. Midlothian Country Club, Blue Island, Illinois, in 1914.

Q. What venue in Georgia was the original site for the Sarazen World Open Championship, first contested in 1994?

A. Legends at Chateau Elan, in Braselton, Georgia.

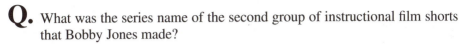

Q. What was the series name of the second group of instructional film shorts that Bobby Jones made?

A. *How to Break 90* (six films).

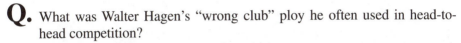

Q. What was Walter Hagen's "wrong club" ploy he often used in head-to-head competition?

A. While waiting for the other golfer to play a shot, Hagen, knowing he was being watched, would pull a certain club from his bag to confuse the other player about his own club selection; then he would replace the club with his real choice after the other guy had hit.

Q. What was the result of the special seventy-two-hole challenge conducted in 1926 between that era's top amateur, Bobby Jones, and the top professional, Walter Hagen?

A. Hagen in a romp, 12 and 11.

Q. How did Jones win back his honor from Hagen later that year (1926)?

A. By beating Hagen et al to win the British Open.

Q. Who was the last golfer to beat Jones in a tournament before Jones officially retired in 1930?

A. Horton Smith, at the 1930 Savannah Open.

Q. How long did Walter Hagen's first marriage, to Margaret (Johnson), last?

A. Four years.

The Jones-Hagen-Sarazen Triumvirate Won at Least One Major Each Year in the Roaring Twenties

(Allowing for a little latitude in 1920)

1920—Jones, U.S. Amateur medalist
1921—Hagen, PGA
1922—Sarazen, U.S. Open and PGA; Hagen, British Open
1923—Jones, U.S. Open; Sarazen, PGA
1924—Jones, U.S. Amateur; Hagen, British Open and PGA
1925—Jones, U.S. Amateur; Hagen, PGA
1926—Jones, U.S. Open and British Open; Hagen, PGA
1927—Jones, U.S. Amateur and British Open; Hagen, PGA
1928—Jones, U.S. Amateur; Hagen, British Open
1929—Jones, U.S. Open; Hagen, British Open

Q. Bobby Jones held college degrees in what three areas of study?

A. English literature, engineering, and law.

Q. Jones's father, also named Robert, was known affectionately by what nickname?

A. Colonel Bob.

Q. Who won the only time Gene Sarazen and Walter Hagen met in the finals of a PGA Championship?

A. Sarazen defeated Hagen, one up after thirty-eight holes, to win the 1923 PGA.

Q. One of the eulogizers at Jones's funeral (he died in 1971) was what golfer who had been Jones's first Walker Cup opponent (in 1922) and his last British Amateur opponent (in 1930)?

A. Roger Wethered.

Q. Walter Hagen defeated what four men in the match-play finals of his four consecutive PGA Championship victories from 1924 to 1927?

A. In order: James Barnes, William Mehlhorn, Leo Diegel, and Joe Turnesa.

Q. How old was Jones when he competed for the first time in the U.S. Amateur?

A. Fourteen, in 1916.

Q. Gene Sarazen's final official tournament victory came in what seniors' event?

A. The 1958 PGA Seniors' Championship.

Q. What cousin of Bobby Jones's went on to great things at Burlington Industries before later becoming the head man of a golf manufacturer that ruled the roost in the mid-nineties?

A. Ely Callaway.

Q. Gene Sarazen was a commentator for what popular TV golf series?

A. Shell's *Wonderful World of Golf*.

Q. What was the disease that gradually disabled Bobby Jones over the last half of his life?

A. Syringomyelia, a debilitating affliction that attacks the spinal cord.

Q. Jones gave what name to his favorite putter?

A. Calamity Jane.

Walter Hagen won four British Open titles and the affections of golf fans around the world, as is evidenced here while he celebrates his 1924 Open triumph at Hoylake, England. (©PHIL SHELDON)

Q. After divorcing his first wife, Hagen, always the ladies' man, carried what page-turner around the world with him?

A. A little black book listing what he called "friendly natives."

Q. In what year did Gene Sarazen finally win his first and only British Open title?

A. 1932.

5

SCORECARD

40 Questions
Par: 3

Correct answers	Score	
40	Ace	1
30–39	Birdie	2
20–29	Par	3
10–19	Bogey	4
Less than 10	Double Bogey	5

Your score _____

6

THE LPGA

70 Questions
Par: 4

Q. How tall is long-hitting Laura Davies?

A. Five-foot-ten.

———⊗⊗⊗———

Q. From 1969 to 1980 what LPGA golfer set a record by making 299 consecutive cuts?

A. Jane Blalock.

———⊗⊗⊗———

Q. Where was Nancy Lopez's first LPGA victory, in 1978, and her thirty-fifth, which in 1987 qualified her for the LPGA Hall of Fame?

A. Both in Sarasota, Florida (1978 Bent Tree Classic and 1987 Sarasota Classic).

———⊗⊗⊗———

Q. Who was the first left-hander to win an LPGA event?

A. Bonnie Bryant, at the 1974 Bill Branch Classic.

———⊗⊗⊗———

Q. What was the original name given to the LPGA's tournament series for players forty and over?

A. The Lilly Legends.

———⊗⊗⊗———

Q. In 1988 what golfer saved the life of a three-year-old boy who had fallen into a residential swimming pool across a fence from where the golfer was trying to qualify for the Standard Register Turquoise Classic?

A. Mary Bea Porter.

Q. Kathy Whitworth's eighty-eighth career victory, her last, came in what tournament?

A. The 1985 United Virginia Bank Classic. Whitworth's victory total remains an American record, male and female.

Q. What biennial transatlantic competition has become to women's golf what the Ryder Cup is to men's?

A. Solheim Cup.

Q. Prior to 1997 who had been the only two LPGA golfers to end a tour event at twenty or more under par?

A. Nancy Lopez (1985 Henredon Classic) and Beth Daniel (1994 Oldsmobile Classic).

Q. What 1998 LPGA rookie graduated cum laude from Yale?

A. Heather Daly-Donofrio.

Q. Already a world champion at track and field and a star at basketball, LPGA Hall of Famer-to-be Babe Zaharias first took up golf at age twenty-one in 1935 at the urging of what notable sports figure?

A. Sportswriter Grantland Rice.

Q. Who was the first native of India to make it onto the LPGA tour?

A. Smriti Mehra, who led the tour in driving distance with an average poke of 263 yards in her rookie season of 1997.

Q. *Jill's Junior Golf Tips*, a children's coloring book, was authored by what LPGA golfer?

A. Jill Briles-Hinton.

Babe Didrickson Zaharias was voted Associated Press Woman Athlete of the First Half of the 20th Century, yet most of her greatest exploits in golf didn't even come until after 1947 and well after her thirtieth birthday. Starting in 1948, the Babe helped launch the LPGA, winning thirty-one events, including three U.S. Women's Opens and two Titleholders Championships. Incredibly, the most money she ever won in one season was just a little under $11,500, that coming in 1954, when she won five events. (COURTESY OF LIBRARY OF CONGRESS)

Q. In a career conspicuously missing a major-tournament triumph, what New Hampshire native won twenty-nine LPGA events?

A. Jane Blalock.

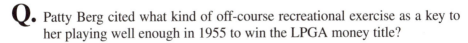

Q. Patty Berg cited what kind of off-course recreational exercise as a key to her playing well enough in 1955 to win the LPGA money title?

A. Tap dancing.

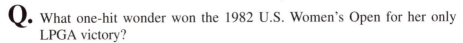

Q. What one-hit wonder won the 1982 U.S. Women's Open for her only LPGA victory?

A. Janet Anderson.

Q. What current LPGA player has scored two USGA tournament hat tricks by winning three U.S. Junior Girls' titles as well as three U.S. Women's Opens?

A. Hollis Stacy.

Q. While attempting a shot from a sidehill lie, what member of the 1998 U.S. Solheim Cup team lost her balance and fell into a water hazard at Muirfield Village?

A. Brandie Burton.

Q. A then-record fine of $3,500 was assessed what golfer for her profane outburst caught by TV cameras at the 1985 LPGA National Pro-Am in Denver?

A. Lori Garbacz.

Q. What American participated in the 1998 Solheim Cup while six months pregnant?

A. Tammie Green.

Q. Why did Dottie Pepper need fifteen stitches in her leg in 1994?

A. She was bitten by her dog Shank.

Q. Laura Davies won what LPGA event four consecutive years?

A. Standard Register Ping.

Q. In 1992 what golfer won the NCAA women's title and the U.S. Women's Amateur, both times beating Annika Sorenstam head-to-head?

A. Vicki Goetze (now Goetze-Ackerman).

Q. The golf world bid farewell in 1998 to what LPGA director of tournament operations, who gallantly fought a seven-and-a-half-year battle with breast cancer?

A. Suzanne Jackson.

Q. In what year were the first Solheim Cup Matches between American women and their European counterparts held?

A. 1990, when the Yanks took an 11½–3½ victory.

Q. Who was the LPGA's first commissioner?

A. Ray Volpe.

Q. The first LPGA golfer to win at least $100,000 in a season was what St. Louis native?

A. Judy Rankin, in 1976.

Q. What was the deal with Carin Hj Koch's middle name?

A. It was an abbreviation of her maiden name, Hjalmarsson.

Q. What three-time winner on the 1990 LPGA circuit was badly burned in a hospitality-tent fire at the 1993 Sara Lee Classic?

A. Cathy Gerring.

Q. Who are the five golfers who qualified for the LPGA Hall of Fame between 1980 and 1998?

A. JoAnne Carner, Nancy Lopez, Pat Bradley, Patty Sheehan, and Betsy King.

Golf Nut Meg

Meg Mallon is one of the LPGA's relatively silent but congenial stars, the winner of both the LPGA Championship and the U.S. Women's Open in 1991 and a consistent leader-board presence who goes about her work with a sincere smile and deadly putting stroke. One of the best-liked players among her peers, Mallon has a fiercely competitive streak she disguises well and a deep appreciation for the rules of the game. At the Jamie Farr Kroger Classic in Ohio in July 1996, Mallon went to bed one night holding the second-round lead. While she was trying to sleep it dawned on her that she might have unwittingly violated a rule during the second round by waiting too long for a putt to drop. When Mallon turned herself in to tournament officials the next day, she was disqualified for having signed an incorrect scorecard that didn't include the penalty stroke she had incurred. The truth hurts, but it does wonders for those sleepless nights.

Q. What flamboyant, big-hitting star of the LPGA is to fancy golf hats what Imelda Marcos was to shoes?

A. Michelle McGann.

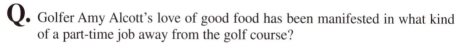

Q. Golfer Amy Alcott's love of good food has been manifested in what kind of a part-time job away from the golf course?

A. Short-order cook at an L.A. sandwich shop.

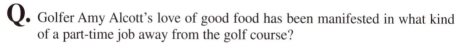

Q. Annika Sorenstam is fluent in what three languages?

A. English, French, and, of course, Swedish.

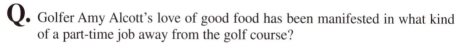

Q. In 1994 who became the first honorary member of the LPGA Hall of Fame?

A. Dinah Shore.

Q. Who was the LPGA's first player to crack the $1 million mark in lifetime earnings?

A. Kathy Whitworth, in 1981.

Q. At age forty-six who won the 1988 Safeco Classic to become the LPGA's oldest winner of a tour event?

A. JoAnne Carner.

Q. What Hall of Fame golfer served as the LPGA's first president?

A. Patty Berg.

Q. By winning the 1997 LPGA Championship, what underrated LPGA veteran and winner of numerous events finally conquered a major?

A. Chris Johnson.

Q. What former first lady is an honorary member of the LPGA?

A. Betty Ford.

Q. What golfer won twenty-four tournaments between 1969 and 1981, including two LPGA Championships and two U.S. Women's Opens, but has been conspicuous by her absence from the admissions-specific LPGA Hall of Fame?

A. Donna Caponi.

Q. What veteran of fourteen years on the LPGA circuit made the 1997 State Farm Rail Classic her first tour victory?

A. Cindy Figg-Currier.

Q. What former Wimbledon and U.S. Open tennis champion later played on the LPGA tour?

A. Althea Gibson, from 1963 to 1977. Her best year money-wise was 1967, when she finished twenty-third on the money list.

Althea Gibson
(COURTESY OF LPGA)

Q. The LPGA's commissioners during the nineties were what four men?

A. Bill Blue, Charlie Mechem, Jim Ritts, and Ty Votaw.

Q. Who was the tour's first player to crack the $1 million mark in a single season?

A. Karrie Webb, in 1996.

Q. The acronym LPGA stands for what, exactly?

A. Ladies Professional Golf Association.

Q. What playing member of the LPGA Hall of Fame retired with fewer than thirty career tour victories?

A. Betty Jameson, an LPGA founder, who went on to capture only ten career victories.

Ten LPGA Winners from the 1980s We Hardly Knew or Barely Remember

Barbara Barrow, 1980 Birmingham Classic
Cathy Reynolds, 1981 Golden Lights Championship
Janet Anderson, 1982 U.S. Women's Open
Lenore Muraoka, 1983 United Virginia Bank Classic
Sally Quinlan, 1984 Mastercard International Pro-Am
Bonnie Lauer, 1985 Uniden LPGA Invitational
Penny Pulz, 1986 Circle K Tucson Open
Cindy Hill, 1987 S&H Golf Classic
Mei-Chi Cheng, 1988 Rochester International
Robin Hood, 1989 Planters Pat Bradley International

Q. What is the name of the award given annually to the LPGA's low scorer?

A. Vare Trophy.

Q. What LPGA Hall of Famer won ten events and the Vare Trophy in 1968, yet finished second on that year's money list?

A. Six-foot-three Carol Mann, who was out-earned by five-foot-ten Kathy Whitworth, who won eleven times.

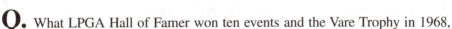

Q. What charter member of the LPGA was only sixteen years old when she joined (1950), yet already held an Associated Press Athlete of the Year award?

A. Marlene Hagge.

Q. Going into the 1999 season, who was the last American to win the LPGA's Player of the Year Award?

A. Beth Daniel, in 1994.

Behind those cool sunglasses and picture-perfect follow-through, **Annika Sorenstam** is, well, one cool-headed golfer with a game about as perfectly consistent as any to be found on the pro tours. (JAN TRAYLEN PHOTO/©PHIL SHELDON)

Q. In the first nine years of the LPGA's Ellen Griffin Rolex Award, which honors an individual making a major contribution to the teaching of golf, who was the only male winner?

A. Harvey Penick, in 1992.

Q. Four years into her semi-retirement, Mickey Wright won what prominent 1973 event?

A. Colgate Dinah Shore Classic.

Q. What underrated player, who competed for relatively few years while starting a family, won three U.S. Opens between 1968 and 1973?

A. Susie Maxwell Berning.

Q. The LPGA Hall of Fame includes among its members what Vermont native?

A. Patty Sheehan.

Q. Who was the last LPGA player (of seven) to tie the tour's single-round scoring record of 62 before Se Ri Pak shot a 61 in 1998?

A. Kristi Albers. Meg Mallon and Albers both shot a 62 in 1998, but Albers scored hers later than Mallon.

Q. Who set an LPGA seventy-two-hole scoring record (broken by Se Ri Pak a year later) by shooting a twenty-three-under 265 at the 1997 Fieldcrest Cannon Classic?

A. Wendy Ward.

Q. The distinction of being the first LPGA player to reach the $2 million, $3 million, and $4 million marks in career earnings belongs to what golfer?

A. Pat Bradley.

Q. Who won thirty-nine times between 1961 and 1976 and notched seven top-three finishes on the money list in her career but never finished a season number one in earnings?

A. Sandra Haynie.

Q. Interstitial cystitis, a painful bladder disorder, has long afflicted what golfer who made a stirring statement of perseverance by winning twice in 1997, when she also won the Heather Farr Award?

A. Terry-Jo Myers.

Q. Who is Annika Sorenstam's younger sister who has also played on the LPGA tour?

A. Charlotta Sorenstam.

Mickey Wright won ten majors and a total of eighty-two tournaments during a spectacular career that reached its apex in the late fifties and early sixties. Tall and strong, Wright had a dream swing that some experts said was as close to ideal as that of any person who ever played the game, male or female. Lingering foot problems, an adverse reaction to sunlight, and her dislike for air travel, however, convinced Wright to stop playing regularly after 1969, even though she was only thirty-four years old at the time. Wright twice won the LPGA Championship and U.S. Women's Open in the same year (1958 and 1961) and added the Titleholders—a third major in those days—to her list in 1961. Between 1959 and 1968 she averaged nearly eight victories a year on the LPGA tour. (©PHIL SHELDON)

Q. The 1988 U.S. Women's Open was what Swedish native's first pro victory on American soil?

A. Liselotte Neumann.

Q. What is Judy Rankin's maiden name?

A. Judy Torluemke.

Ten Offbeat Hobbies and Interests of LPGA Players
(Or so they claim in the 1998 LPGA Media Guide)

1. Jumping over rose gardens, Jill McGill
2. Crown green bowling, Joanne Morley
3. Fast roller coasters, Susie Redman
4. Collecting Precious Moments and Robert Raikes Bears, Kathy Guadagnino
5. Singing in the shower, Jill McGill
6. Deep-sea fishing, Cristie Kerr
7. Flying kites, Karen Davies
8. Fox hunting, Muffin Spencer-Devlin
9. Snorkeling, JoAnne Carner
10. Throwing darts, Jill McGill

(Obviously, McGill wanted the attention. She got it.)

Q. The annual LPGA event that involves team play matching the United States against Japan has what name?

A. The Nichirei International.

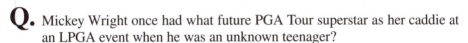

Q. Mickey Wright once had what future PGA Tour superstar as her caddie at an LPGA event when he was an unknown teenager?

A. Paul Azinger.

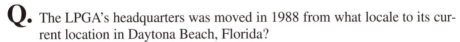

Q. The LPGA's headquarters was moved in 1988 from what locale to its current location in Daytona Beach, Florida?

A. Sugar Land, Texas.

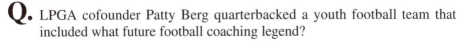

Q. LPGA cofounder Patty Berg quarterbacked a youth football team that included what future football coaching legend?

A. Bud Wilkinson.

Q. Fifteen years went by before what African-American woman became the first black golfer since Renee Powell retired in 1980 to play the LPGA tour?

A. LaRee Pearl Sugg, a tour rookie in 1995.

Q. What tour veteran and former *Fairway* magazine player/model ended a fifteen-year drought between victories by winning the 1995 Oldsmobile Classic?

A. Dale Eggeling.

Q. Who won the first LPGA Championship?

A. Beverly Hanson, in 1955.

Q. What two LPGA stars in the 1999 season gained entry into the Hall of Fame, thanks to new admission criteria?

A. Beth Daniel and Amy Alcott.

6

SCORECARD

70 Questions
Par: 4

Correct answers	Score	
68–70	Eagle	2
50–67	Birdie	3
35–49	Par	4
25–34	Bogey	5
10–24	Double Bogey	6
Less than 10	Triple Bogey	7

Your score _____

60 Questions
Par: 4

Q. What emerging golf star was born in Finland, is a naturalized Swedish citizen, has owned a home in Monaco, and shows his admiration of Arnold Schwarzenegger by signing "the Terminator" as part of his autograph?

A. Jarmo Sandelin.

Q. What event is considered the most prestigious major event on the European PGA Tour?

A. Its PGA Championship, most recently sponsored by Volvo.

Q. In what city is the annual holiday-season Million Dollar Challenge held?

A. Sun City, Bophuthatswana.

Q. Who was the first American accorded captain honors at Scotland's prestigious Royal and Ancient Golf Club?

A. Francis Ouimet, in 1951.

Q. What is the proper name of the European PGA Tour's annual money list?

A. The European Order of Merit.

Q. Who was the first male Japanese golfer to win on the U.S. tour?

A. Isao Aoki, at the 1983 Hawaiian Open.

———∞———

Q. Hale Irwin and Raymond Floyd were among those defeated by what easy-going Aussie for the 1977 World Matchplay title?

A. Graham Marsh.

———∞———

Q. Hale Irwin was vanquished in the 1976 World Matchplay by what native Australian, who took thirty-eight holes to finish off the bespectacled one in a thrilling final?

A. David Graham.

———∞———

Q. What former Masters winner has been linked with plans to construct a golf course near the Great Wall of China?

A. Ian Woosnam.

———∞———

Q. Spaniard Seve Ballesteros saw his U.S. PGA Tour membership revoked in 1985 for what reason?

A. As an active globetrotter, he divided his time among several tours but failed to play in the minimum fifteen PGA Tour events needed to maintain his card.

———∞———

Q. Who was the first American to reach the summit of the World Rankings, instituted in the mid-1980s?

A. Fred Couples, in 1992.

———∞———

Q. What native Australian golfer (who later moved to Dallas) named his oil-exploration company *Cockatoo*?

A. Bruce Crampton.

Q. What refreshingly candid native Scotsman won his sixth consecutive European Order of Merit title in 1998?

A. Colin Montgomerie.

———∞———

Q. A frequent contender on the Senior PGA Tour in the late 1990s and runner-up to Hale Irwin at the 1998 U.S. Senior Open was what Argentina native?

A. Vicente Fernandez.

———∞———

Q. Harry Vardon and Ted Ray, winners of seven British Open Championships between them, were both born where?

A. Jersey, England.

———∞———

Q. What two European golf superstars had children born on the same day in the same hospital in March 1993?

A. Nick Faldo and Colin Montgomerie.

———∞———

Q. The Australian Open was won by whom in both 1992 and 1994?

A. Robert Allenby.

———∞———

Q. What amateur women's team competition between Great Britain–Ireland and the United States is held every two years?

A. Curtis Cup.

———∞———

Q. In 1998 what Australian golfer's wife/caddie was killed in a freak accident?

A. Stuart Appleby. Renay Appleby was pinned between two cars while unloading luggage from a taxicab outside London's Waterloo Station.

Q. What American has never ended a year ranked higher than sixth in the world, even after five consecutive top-nine finishes on the PGA Tour money list from 1989 through 1993 and a 1993 season with ten top-three tournament finishes, including victories at the Memorial and the PGA Championshp, less than a year after he had won the Tour Championship?

A. Paul Azinger.

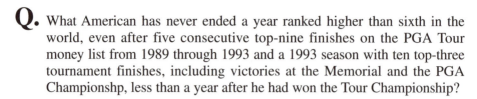

Q. Foreigners won both the Masters and U.S. Open for the first time in what year?

A. 1994; José Maria Olazábal and Ernie Els, respectively.

Q. Dave Barr, Richard Zokol, and Dan Halldorson have what in common in terms of native geography, eh?

A. All hail from Canada.

Q. Controversy over where the sport of golf originated usually centers on what two countries?

A. Scotland and Holland.

Q. What native South African and Senior PGA Tour veteran is perhaps best known for the goofy little waist-high wave he gives while backing away after sinking a birdie or otherwise significant putt?

A. Harold Henning.

Q. Between 1988 and 1994 foreigners won six of seven LPGA Rookie of the Year Awards, with the one American exception being what golfer?

A. Brandie Burton, in 1991.

Few will argue that South African **Ernie Els** owns one of the smoothest swings in golf, but he can reshape himself into a nifty shotmaker when the circumstances present themselves, as pictured here in the 1998 Dubai Desert Classic.

(©PHIL SHELDON)

Q. Who was the first American after Bill Rogers (in 1979) to win the World Matchplay title?

A. Corey Pavin, in 1993.

Q. In the late 1970s, what future European Solheim Cup team captain was one of the first Swedes to come to America to play collegiate golf?

A. Pia Nilsson, at Arizona State.

Q. Senior PGA Tour player John Bland, the Tour's Rookie of the Year in 1996, hails from what country?

A. South Africa.

Q. What Spanish teenage sensation of the late 1990s was dubbed "El Niño"?

A. Sergio Garcia.

Q. In what year was the Royal and Ancient Golf Club at St. Andrews, Scotland, founded?

A. 1754.

Q. His victory at the 1976 Dutch Open was the first of nine different nations' open championships for what golfer?

A. Seve Ballesteros, who would like to make the U.S. Open number ten.

Q. Vijay Singh, winner of the 1998 PGA and 2000 Masters, is a native of what island nation?

A. Fiji.

Q. What South African woman won three LPGA majors during the 1980s and finished in the top ten on that tour's money list every year from 1978 through 1982?

A. Sally Little.

Q. A tragic accident that nearly killed him in 1983 ended the pro-tour career of what budding international star who had been the runner-up at the 1975 British Open?

A. Australian Jack Newton, who lost his right eye and right arm when he accidentally walked into the propeller of a small airplane.

Q. Jesper Parnevik's dad is what kind of celebrity in his own right?

A. Bo Parnevik is one of Sweden's most popular comedians.

Q. How was Nick Faldo faring at the 1994 Alfred Dunhill Masters when he was disqualified for removing a piece of coral from his bunkered ball?

A. He was leading by six shots.

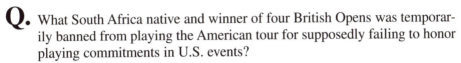

Q. What South Africa native and winner of four British Opens was temporarily banned from playing the American tour for supposedly failing to honor playing commitments in U.S. events?

A. Bobby Locke. Another version of the story alleges that Locke was banned because he was too good a player.

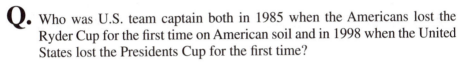

Q. Who was U.S. team captain both in 1985 when the Americans lost the Ryder Cup for the first time on American soil and in 1998 when the United States lost the Presidents Cup for the first time?

A. Jack Nicklaus.

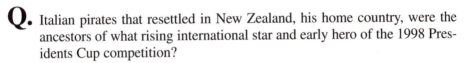

Q. Italian pirates that resettled in New Zealand, his home country, were the ancestors of what rising international star and early hero of the 1998 Presidents Cup competition?

A. Frank Nobilo.

Q. Who is "Popeye"?

A. Australian Craig Parry, thick forearms and all.

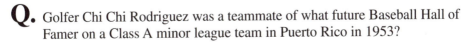

Q. What global star was born in South Africa, grew up in what is now known as Zimbabwe, carries a British passport, and has a home in Florida?

A. Nick Price.

———∞———

Q. Golfer Chi Chi Rodriguez was a teammate of what future Baseball Hall of Famer on a Class A minor league team in Puerto Rico in 1953?

A. Roberto Clemente.

Q. What six-foot-eight European played a major role in leading the Great Britain-and-Ireland team to victory over the Tiger Woods–led U.S. team in the 1995 Walker Cup Matches?

A. Gordon Sherry.

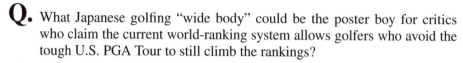

Q. What Japanese golfing "wide body" could be the poster boy for critics who claim the current world-ranking system allows golfers who avoid the tough U.S. PGA Tour to still climb the rankings?

A. Masashi "Jumbo" Ozaki.

Q. What three golfers have led both the U.S. and European PGA Tour money lists?

A. Billy Casper, Gary Player, and Greg Norman.

Q. In the mid-1990s what media organization was the money behind Greg Norman's bold but failed attempt to launch a World Tour?

A. Fox Television.

Q. Television golf announcer David Feherty hails from what country?

A. Northern Ireland.

Q. The last time a native golfer won the Canadian Open was 1954, when what Canadian won his national open?

A. Pat Fletcher.

Q. Who were the opposing team captains in the inaugural Presidents Cup, contested in 1994?

A. David Graham for the Internationals and Hale Irwin for the winning Yanks.

Q. What American, the 1998 British Open runner-up, has spent much of his professional career plying his trade in Asia instead of the United States?

A. Brian Watts.

———— ⦿ ————

Q. Why did South African David Frost drop his drawers in plain sight during the 1994 Presidents Cup?

A. He was stung by a wasp that had crawled inside his pants.

———— ⦿ ————

Q. Often called "that other guy from Zimbabwe" (other than Nick Price, that is), what longtime PGA European Tour mainstay finished second to Nick Faldo at the 1990 British Open at St. Andrews?

A. Mark McNulty, born in Zimbabwe and with residences in South Africa and England.

———— ⦿ ————

Q. What fiery American solidified her unofficial status as "the Seve of the Solheim" by posting a 4-0 match-play record in the United States's 1998 Solheim Cup victory over Europe?

A. Dottie Pepper.

———— ⦿ ————

Q. Spaniard José Maria Olazábal can be forgiven for having visions of Greg Norman when he thinks about his lingering foot problems that were finally cured, in part, by injections of what substance?

A. Shark cartilage.

———— ⦿ ————

Q. What leader, who assumed control of his government in 1997, is said to have shot a round of 34 (38 under par for *eighteen* holes) that included four aces?

A. North Korea's Kim Jong Il, who, nonetheless, needn't hold his breath waiting for a special Masters invite from the suits at Augusta.

A Dozen Different Nations Represented by Major Tournament Winners of the 1990s

Player	Home Country	Major Victory(ies)
Nick Faldo	England	1990, 1996 Masters; 1990, 1992 British Open
Ian Woosnam	Wales	1991 Masters
Nick Price	Zimbabwe	1992, 1994 PGA; 1994 British Open
Bernhard Langer	Germany	1993 Masters
José Maria Olazábal	Spain	1994, 1999 Masters
Ernie Els	South Africa	1994, 1997 U.S. Open
Annika Sorenstam	Sweden	1995, 1996 U.S. Women's Open
Jenny Lidback	Peru	1995 du Maurier Classic
Steve Elkington	Australia	1995 PGA
Tiger Woods	"Cablinasia" (U.S.)	1997 Masters, 1999 PGA
Se Ri Pak	Korea	1998 U.S. Women's Open, LPGA
Vijay Singh	Fiji	1998 PGA

Q. What prominent Senior PGA Tour golfer had his caddie carry him back and forth across a river at the 1967 Carling World Championships so he could play his next shot without penalty (and with dry feet) after badly slicing his tee shot?

A. Chi Chi Rodriguez, all 130 or so pounds of him.

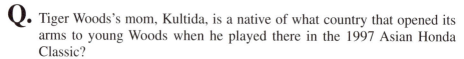

Q. At St. Andrews in a 1997 Dunhill Cup semifinal against American Justin Leonard, what Swedish golfer shot a front-nine 27?

A. Joakim Haeggman.

Q. Tiger Woods's mom, Kultida, is a native of what country that opened its arms to young Woods when he played there in the 1997 Asian Honda Classic?

A. Thailand.

Q. In 1997 what New Zealand native and third-place finisher in the 1995 British Open claimed that he purposely missed cuts on the European PGA Tour but retracted his statements the next day?

A. Michael Campbell.

———— ⧉ ————

Q. Swedish golfer Jesper Parnevik follows a diet that includes what substance that he claims makes him play better?

A. Volcanic sand.

SCORECARD

60 Questions
Par: 4

Correct answers	Score	
58–60	Eagle	2
45–57	Birdie	3
30–44	Par	4
20–29	Bogey	5
10–19	Double Bogey	6
Less than 10	Triple Bogey	7

Your score _____

8

AUGUSTA

90 Questions
Par: 5

Q. Who succeeded Jackson Stephens as chairman of Augusta National and the Masters Tournament?

A. William "Hootie" Johnson.

Q. What golfer was caught sneaking friends into the 1989 Masters in the trunk of his courtesy car?

A. Ken Green, who was nabbed when his brother-in-law was caught on the course without the requisite spectator's badge.

Q. What stream winds its way through Augusta National?

A. Rae's Creek.

Q. What winner of multiple Masters Tournaments is honored with a plaque near Augusta's sixteenth hole and a seven-foot statue of himself in downtown Augusta?

A. Arnold Palmer.

Q. What U.S. Army post is located on the outskirts of Augusta, Georgia?

A. Fort Gordon.

Q. A tradition in and around Augusta during Masters week is what kind of betting-pool party?

A. Calcutta, officially banned by the USGA in 1948 and illegal in Georgia.

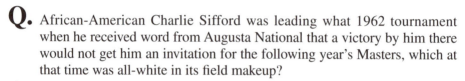

Q. What Augusta businessman and Masters ticket broker committed suicide during Masters week in 1997 after he was unable to fulfill orders of Masters badges promised to rich, high-powered customers?

A. Allen Caldwell III.

Q. African-American Charlie Sifford was leading what 1962 tournament when he received word from Augusta National that a victory by him there would not get him an invitation for the following year's Masters, which at that time was all-white in its field makeup?

A. The Canadian Open; Sifford eventually relinquished his lead; Ted Kroll went on to win.

Q. Although long deceased, Bobby Jones still carries what title at Augusta National?

A. President in Perpetuity.

Q. Although he notched three top-five Masters finishes between 1967 and 1971 and handcrafted models of Augusta National's greens to scale in his home, what golfer never won a green jacket?

A. Bert Yancey.

Q. The Masters trophy is a solid silver replica of what landmark?

A. Augusta National's clubhouse.

Q. In what year was Augusta's par-three course built?

A. 1958.

Q. In the early fifties Augusta National's inner circle supported Dwight Eisenhower's bid for the presidency by forming what political action committee?

A. Citizens for Eisenhower.

Q. What rendered CBS-TV golf anchor Jim Nantz speechless, literally, the day before the start of the 1997 Masters?

A. A wicked case of pollen-induced allergies.

Q. What golf-loving billionaire began 1999 still waiting for his coveted invitation to join Augusta National, although he had code-named one of his company's new building-construction projects as Augusta?

A. Bill Gates.

Q. Clifford Roberts and a group of Augusta members sponsored what black prizefighter and local shoeshine man to fight in New York?

A. Beau Jack.

Q. Even after making his double eagle in the final round of the 1935 Masters, before claiming victory, Gene Sarazen had to tough out a thirty-six-hole play-off against whom?

A. Craig Wood.

Q. During the 1997 pre-Masters Par-3 Contest, what rocker with ties to the Eagles caddied for Brad Faxon?

A. Glenn Frey.

Q. What was the first year Masters participants were allowed to bring in their own caddies?

A. 1983.

The Augusta National clubhouse that graces the end of Magnolia Lane is a stately manor to be respected by all those who enter there. (©PHIL SHELDON)

Q. What was the lowest eighteen-hole score club cofounder Bobby Jones notched in his dozen Masters appearances?

A. 72—he never broke par.

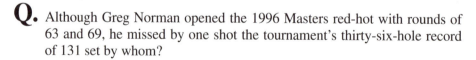

Q. Although Greg Norman opened the 1996 Masters red-hot with rounds of 63 and 69, he missed by one shot the tournament's thirty-six-hole record of 131 set by whom?

A. Raymond Floyd, who went on to win the 1976 Masters with a then-record 271 total.

Q. Through 1998 what three amateurs had won the Par-3 Contest preceding the Masters?

A. Deane Beman (1961), Labron Harris Jr. (1964), and Jay Haas (1976).

Q. Whose 75 was the highest opening-round score ever shot by a Masters winner-to-be?

A. Craig Stadler, in 1982.

———⊗⊗⊗———

Q. What is the name of the main airport servicing Augusta, Georgia?

A. Bush Field.

———⊗⊗⊗———

Q. What potentially dangerous incident occurred at Augusta National in October 1983 while President Ronald Reagan was playing golf there?

A. Charles Harris, a lone gunman, crashed through Augusta's gates, took hostages in the pro shop, and demanded an audience with Reagan. He was subdued before he could meet the Gipper.

———⊗⊗⊗———

Q. What Okie whose career Masters amateur record of three top-ten finishes and six low-amateur awards remains unrivaled?

A. Charlie Coe.

———⊗⊗⊗———

Q. The Augusta powers have deemed off limits for on-air mention by CBS-TV golf announcers what one subject most pertinent to all *pro* golf tournaments?

A. Money.

———⊗⊗⊗———

Q. The city of Augusta's minor league baseball team has what nickname?

A. The Green Jackets.

———⊗⊗⊗———

Q. Who was the first Augusta, Georgia, native to win the Masters?

A. Larry Mize, in 1987.

Q. Augusta National cofounder and president Clifford Roberts used what kind of weapon to commit suicide in 1977?

A. Smith & Wesson .38 pistol.

Q. Roberts refused CBS-TV's offer to use what variety-show host to open the 1966 Masters telecasts with a thirty-second spot about the tournament's limited-commercials policy?

A. Ed Sullivan.

Q. What interstate highway connecting Atlanta and Columbia, South Carolina, runs through Augusta, Georgia?

A. I-20.

Q. After Hubert Green missed a three-foot, sidehill putt in the 1978 Masters that would have put him in a play-off with Gary Player, Green returned to the eighteenth green and sank how many of his five attempts at the same putt?

A. None.

Q. Who was the first golfer to get his first United States victory at the Masters?

A. Bernhard Langer, in 1985.

Q. The dad of what prominent teaching pro with a client list that has included Greg Norman and Tiger Woods won the Masters in 1948?

A. Butch Harmon, whose dad was Claude Harmon.

Q. What was the "après-golf" card game of choice for the likes of Ike, Cliff, and the boys back at the clubhouse?

A. Bridge.

Q. Security guards on-site at the Masters traditionally come from what company?

A. Pinkerton's.

Q. What Masters champion punctuated his victory with a dramatic sand-blast birdie at the last hole?

A. Doug Ford, in 1957.

Q. Who was the first recipient of a Masters Tournament green jacket?

A. Sam Snead, in 1949 (the first year the winner got a green jacket).

Q. Bobby Jones and Clifford Roberts formed what company to bottle Coca-Cola in South America?

A. Joroberts, Inc.

Q. What three holes comprise Augusta's Amen Corner?

A. Eleven, twelve, and thirteen.

Q. Who gave the name *Amen Corner* to that three-hole stretch on Augusta's back nine?

A. Grantland Rice, sportswriter and Augusta member.

Q. Augusta merchants and citizens organized what prominent social event for many years preceding the Masters Tournament?

A. The Golf Ball.

Q. Augusta National's green jacket contains what fiber mixture?

A. 55 percent wool, 45 percent polyester.

Ten Notables from Other Walks of Life Who Have Been Augusta National Members

1. Ty Cobb, baseball star
2. Grantland Rice, sportswriter
3. Dwight D. Eisenhower, U.S. president
4. Frank Broyles, college football coach and athletic director
5. Ron Townsend, CBS-TV affiliate owner and first black member
6. Warren Buffett, billionaire
7. E. F. Hutton, who made people listen
8. Alistair Cooke, British journalist
9. Robert Woodruff, Coca-Cola CEO
10. Bud Maytag, washing machines

Q. After trailing by nine shots going into the last round, who won the 1956 Masters?

A. Jack Burke.

Q. Augusta National member Jock Whitney invested millions of dollars in what film classic-to-be?

A. *Gone With the Wind.*

Q. What is the nickname of Augusta's thirteenth hole?

A. Azalea, many of which can be found in April, especially along the thirteenth fairway.

Q. What Canadian golfer was the first foreigner to finish seventy-two holes under par in a Masters Tournament?

A. Stan Leonard, who tied for fourth at two-under 286 in 1958.

Q. In what hotel were the Calcutta betting pools formally held before they were outlawed (at least officially)?

A. Bon Air Vanderbilt.

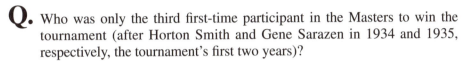

Q. Who was only the third first-time participant in the Masters to win the tournament (after Horton Smith and Gene Sarazen in 1934 and 1935, respectively, the tournament's first two years)?

A. Fuzzy Zoeller, in 1979.

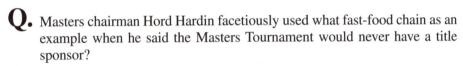

Q. Masters chairman Hord Hardin facetiously used what fast-food chain as an example when he said the Masters Tournament would never have a title sponsor?

A. Pizza Hut.

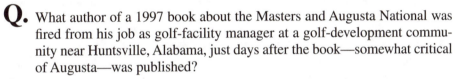

Q. What author of a 1997 book about the Masters and Augusta National was fired from his job as golf-facility manager at a golf-development community near Huntsville, Alabama, just days after the book—somewhat critical of Augusta—was published?

A. Steve Eubanks, author of *Augusta: Home of the Masters Tournament.*

Q. What street runs by the main entrance to Augusta National?

A. Washington Road.

Q. What popular tournament-scoring system for leader boards was initiated by the Masters Tournament, circa 1960?

A. Scores relative to par, with red numbers indicating how many under par; black, how many over.

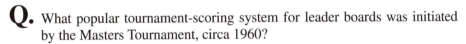

Q. Clifford Roberts was born in what midwestern town?

A. Morning Sun, Iowa.

Strange but True

Two Augusta National members were forced to resign in 1994 after it was learned that they had taken advantage of their status by selling guest rounds of golf to the club for $5,000 apiece. Their biggest blunder that led to their downfall? Advertising their pay-for-play services in the classifieds of a Jacksonville newspaper whose publisher was an Augusta National member.

Q. Briefly hospitalized between the second and third rounds of the 1952 event, what Masters contestant climbed out of bed to win?

A. Jimmy Demaret.

Q. What Augusta National member is best known for his association with another prominent golf club that hosted the 1990 PGA Championship?

A. Hall Thompson, who suffered a PR disaster in the days leading up to the 1990 PGA when he was quoted in a newspaper story regarding Shoal Creek's racist membership policy.

Q. What legendary soul singer hails from Augusta, Georgia?

A. James Brown.

Q. Who was the first native Texan to win the Masters?

A. Byron Nelson, in 1937.

Q. While the golf course was temporarily closed during World War II, what cheap labor cut the grass at Augusta National?

A. Two hundred head of Hereford cattle.

Augusta National cofounder **Clifford Roberts** ruled his roost with an iron fist and rarely a smile.

(©PHIL SHELDON)

Q. What Asian golfer had his special invitation to the 1988 Masters revoked when Augusta officials learned of his alleged association with a crime syndicate?

A. Masashi "Jumbo" Ozaki, of Japan. USGA officials, however, allowed Ozaki to stay in the field of the U.S. Open later that year because Ozaki had not actually been charged with a crime.

Q. What Reagan cabinet official in 1987 racked up an $8,000 tab, at taxpayers' expense, for a three-day golf weekend at Augusta for him and his support staff?

A. Secretary of State George Schultz. The bill went unpaid until an Augusta innkeeper complained to his congressman.

Q. Augusta and Masters Tournament gate-crasher Allen W. Perkins, posing as a contestant at the 1958 Masters, was caught when he performed what flagrant Clifford Roberts no-no?

A. Hitting *five* practice shots into the first green in a practice round. (Roberts's steadfast rule was one ball and one shot at a time.)

———✇———

Q. On what hole at Augusta can (Byron) Nelson's Bridge be found?

A. The thirteenth.

———✇———

Q. Who designed Augusta's par-three course?

A. George Cobb.

———✇———

Q. What past Masters winner was the catalyst behind the establishment of the Champions Dinner, an annual Masters-week event started in 1952?

A. Ben Hogan.

———✇———

Q. Augusta National member Freeman Gosden was the cocreator of what popular radio show?

A. *Amos 'n' Andy.*

———✇———

Q. Who was the first Masters contestant to break 30 on one of Augusta's nines?

A. Mark Calcavecchia, who had a back-nine 29 in the fourth round of the 1992 Masters.

———✇———

Q. Sam Snead for many years performed what physical feat at the Champions Dinner, showing off just how limber he was?

A. Kicking the top of a door frame.

Strange but True

Any serious golf fan born before 1960 knows the unfortunate plight of Roberto De Vicenzo at the 1968 Masters. The Argentinean tied Bob Goalby for the lead after 72 holes to apparently force a play-off, only to sign a final-round scorecard that showed a 4 for the seventeenth hole, where he actually had made a 3. The signing snafu added a stroke to De Vicenzo's total score and gave Goalby the green jacket outright. De Vicenzo graciously blamed himself, although part of the blame has to go to his playing partner that day, Tommy Aaron. Aaron kept De Vicenzo's scorecard and was responsible for the penciling in of the errant 4. Ironically, Aaron won the Masters five years later for his only major-tournament triumph, while De Vicenzo never won a major on American soil (although he had won the 1967 British Open).

Q. The property on which Augusta National is situated occupies how many acres?

A. 365.

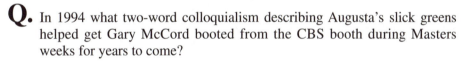

Q. In 1994 what two-word colloquialism describing Augusta's slick greens helped get Gary McCord booted from the CBS booth during Masters weeks for years to come?

A. "Bikini wax."

Q. In what building does the traditional post-Masters victory interview take place?

A. The Butler Cabin.

Q. Why did Masters competitor Ken Venturi put on his sweat-inducing rain pants for two holes on a hot, sunny day in 1968?

A. Modesty. He had split his trousers lining up a putt and had to wait until the turn to change his pants.

Q. Lee Elder had to win a play-off against what player to win the 1974 Monsanto Open and therefore become the first African American to qualify for the Masters Tournament?

A. Peter Oosterhuis.

Lee Elder

(©PHIL SHELDON)

Q. Greg Norman's opening-round 63 in the 1996 Masters tied the tournament single-round record held by whom?

A. Nick Price, who had shot a final-round 63 in 1986.

Q. By what event title was the Masters Tournament originally known?

A. The Augusta National Invitation.

Q. In what year did the tournament's name change take place?

A. 1938.

Q. By what silent means do Augusta National members learn that they have been reclassified as ex-members?

A. Their club bills quit coming.

Q. How did Lee Elder do in 1975 as the first African American ever to compete in the Masters?

A. He missed the cut, shooting 74 and 78.

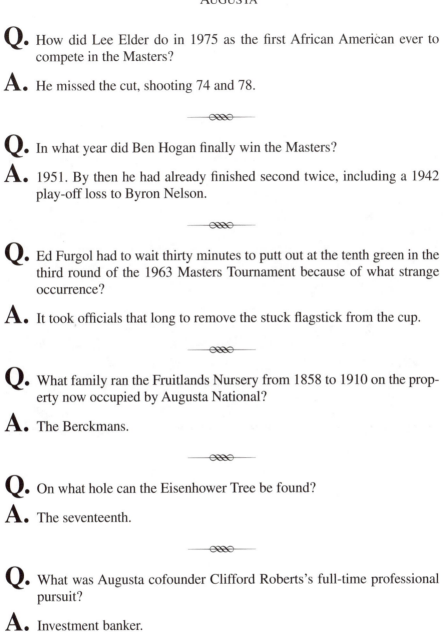

Q. In what year did Ben Hogan finally win the Masters?

A. 1951. By then he had already finished second twice, including a 1942 play-off loss to Byron Nelson.

Q. Ed Furgol had to wait thirty minutes to putt out at the tenth green in the third round of the 1963 Masters Tournament because of what strange occurrence?

A. It took officials that long to remove the stuck flagstick from the cup.

Q. What family ran the Fruitlands Nursery from 1858 to 1910 on the property now occupied by Augusta National?

A. The Berckmans.

Q. On what hole can the Eisenhower Tree be found?

A. The seventeenth.

Q. What was Augusta cofounder Clifford Roberts's full-time professional pursuit?

A. Investment banker.

Q. Augusta National also was the site for the first and second editions of what other major tournament?

A. The PGA Seniors' Championship, first held in 1937.

A Precedent for Roberto's Clemency?

Eight years before Roberto De Vicenzo's scoring snafu at the 1968 Masters cost him a shot at a play-off with declared winner Bob Goalby, golfer Dow Finsterwald was allowed a scoring reprieve that should have set some kind of favorable precedent for De Vicenzo. In this instance Finsterwald shot an opening-round 69 in the 1960 Masters to get into contention. The next day, while paired with Billy Casper, Finsterwald was preparing to hit a practice putt or two on a green after holing out when Casper intervened and stopped him. Casper said it was against the rules to hit practice putts, to which Finsterwald responded by saying he had done it during his round the day before and wasn't aware that it was a problem. Finsterwald thus incurred a two-stroke penalty during his first round, which would then have been a 71 instead of a 69, which would then mean he had signed an incorrect scorecard. Disqualification, right? Wrong. Lenient tournament officials, noting that the no-putting rule was merely a local rule, allowed Finsterwald to change his first-round score without further punishment. "What I did was a breach of the rules and no doubt about it," Finsterwald said. "I just never looked at the back of the scorecard." Tell that to De Vicenzo.

Q. Who was Augusta's first club professional, hand-picked by Bobby Jones?

A. Ed Dudley.

Q. Who was the first African-American member expelled from Augusta?

A. Bill Simms, who had been the second black to join.

Q. What official Augusta National photographer coauthored the 1996 photo history, *Augusta National and the Masters*?

A. Frank Christian Jr.

Q. Who was the second African American to play in the Masters?

A. Jim Thorpe.

Q. Reigning Masters winner Tiger Woods selected what menu for the 1998 Masters' Champions Dinner?

A. Cheeseburgers, french fries, and milk shakes.

8

SCORECARD

90 Questions
Par: 5

Correct answers	Score	
87–90	Double eagle	2
80–86	Eagle	3
65–79	Birdie	4
45–64	Par	5
30–44	Bogey	6
15–29	Double Bogey	7
Less than 15	Triple Bogey	8

Your score _____

9

THE SEVENTIES

60 Questions
Par: 4

Q. What kind of a golf club did astronaut Alan Shepard use to hit shots on the moon during the Apollo 14 mission in 1971?

A. Six-iron.

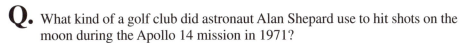

Q. What future U.S. Open champion and future Masters winner, both long-time owners of facial hair, were college teammates at Southern Cal in the early seventies?

A. Scott Simpson and Craig Stadler, respectively.

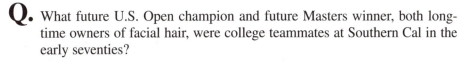

Q. Why did Hubert Green rate an armed escort during the last round of the 1977 U.S. Open, at Southern Hills?

A. Some nut phoned in a death threat, but Green, notified of the threat midway through the back nine, toughed it out to win.

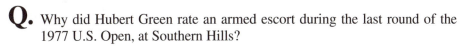

Q. The 1973 Florida Citrus Open was won by what decorated Vietnam vet whose gallery included former POWs?

A. Buddy Allin.

———⊗⊗⊗———

Q. What was the original name of The Players Championship, first contested in 1974?

A. The Tournament Players Championship.

Q. Tom Weiskopf's only pre-Senior Tour major victory came in what event?

A. The 1973 British Open.

Q. Who was the first freshman to win the NCAA men's individual golf title?

A. Ben Crenshaw, in 1971, for the University of Texas.

Q. What 1979 golf book, authored by Timothy Gallwey, was considered innovative because it was an instructional book based on the mental aspects of golf?

A. *The Inner Game of Golf.*

Q. At what golf course did Jack Nicklaus win the 1972 U.S. Open, thus becoming the first man to win the Open and a U.S. Amateur on the same course?

A. Pebble Beach.

Q. In 1973 the LPGA was sued for $2 million by what golfer who had been suspended over alleged cheating?

A. Jane Blalock, who settled out of court.

Q. The Legends of Golf Tournament, first contested in 1978 and the forerunner of what became the Senior PGA Tour, was created by what visionary?

A. Fred Raphael.

Q. What TV golf producer won an Emmy in 1975 for his network?

A. CBS's Frank Chirkinian, for his coverage of the 1975 Masters.

Q. The PGA Tour's headquarters were moved in 1979 from what locale to Ponte Vedra Beach, Florida?

A. Washington, D.C.

Q. What cigar chomper won the 1975 PGA Seniors' Championship?

A. Charlie Sifford.

Q. In 1977, a year before rookie Nancy Lopez won nine tour events, including five in a row, what LPGA veteran, previously winless, had a nice run of her own, winning five times in a four-month span?

A. Debbie Austin.

Q. What golfer who won the 1972 Tournament of Champions in a play-off over Jack Nicklaus was sometimes referred to as "the invisible man"?

A. Bobby Mitchell, who himself even said, "Sometimes I don't even know I'm out there."

Q. In what 1975 PGA Tour event did Johnny Miller notch a fourteen-shot victory?

A. Phoenix Open.

Q. Before Tiger Woods in 1997, who was the last golfer named Associated Press Male Athlete of the Year?

A. Lee Trevino, in 1971.

Q. Which one of Nancy Lopez's nine victories in her incredible rookie year of 1978 came in a major?

A. The LPGA Championship.

Q. Jack Nicklaus failed to win a PGA Tour event in 1979, thus ending a record-tying streak of how many years with at least one tour victory?

A. Seventeen, also accomplished by Arnold Palmer.

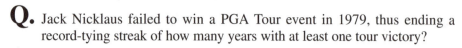

Q. Who was the only woman golfer to win at least two majors in the same year during the seventies?

A. Sandra Haynie, in 1974, who won that year's only two LPGA majors—the U.S. Women's Open and the LPGA Championship.

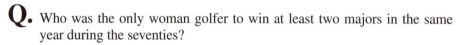

Q. The World Golf Hall of Fame was originally opened in 1974 at what locale?

A. Pinehurst, North Carolina.

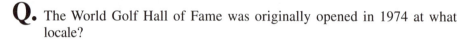

Q. What Wake Forest golfer won the 1979 NCAA golf title and was PGA Tour Rookie of the Year the next year?

A. Gary Hallberg.

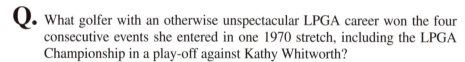

Q. What golfer with an otherwise unspectacular LPGA career won the four consecutive events she entered in one 1970 stretch, including the LPGA Championship in a play-off against Kathy Whitworth?

A. Shirley Englehorn.

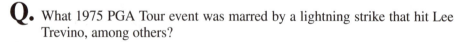

Q. What 1975 PGA Tour event was marred by a lightning strike that hit Lee Trevino, among others?

A. The Western Open. The incident later prompted Trevino to quip that "even God can't hit a one-iron."

Q. What golfer's victory in a U.S. Open contested in the seventies came in his first event after turning pro?

A. Jerry Pate.

Q. In what year did the du Maurier Classic become the LPGA's fourth major?

A. 1979, although in those days it was called the Peter Jackson Classic.

Q. Gene Littler punctuated his comeback from what serious health problem by winning the 1973 St. Louis Children's Hospital Classic?

A. Cancer.

Q. In 1972 the USGA moved its headquarters to what current site?

A. Far Hills, New Jersey.

Q. How many times did a "Tom W." finish first or second in the Masters during the seventies?

A. Six. Tom Watson won in 1977 and was runner-up in 1978 and 1979; Tom Weiskopf was second in 1972, 1974, and 1975.

Q. Arnold Palmer's last top-ten finish on the PGA Tour money list came in what year?

A. 1971.

Q. Who were the only two non-Americans to win the British Open during the 1970s?

A. Gary Player (1974) and Seve Ballesteros (1979).

Q. Who was the first player to shoot his age in an official PGA Tour event?

A. Sam Snead, who, at the age of sixty-seven, shot rounds of 66 and 67 in the 1979 Quad Cities Open.

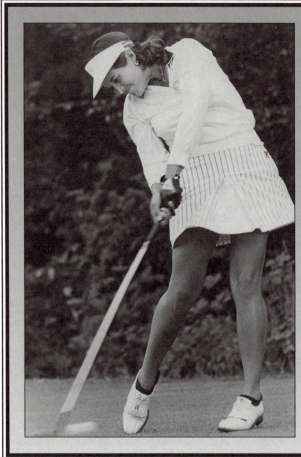

Nancy Lopez gave the LPGA a nice boost when she came out in 1978 as a rookie and won nine events that year, including five in a row. Here she's pictured teeing off on her way to victory in the 1979 Colgate European Open at Sunningdale in England.

(©PHIL SHELDON)

Q. The U.S. Amateur returned to a match-play format in 1973 after eight years of stroke play and was promptly won by what golfer?

A. Craig Stadler.

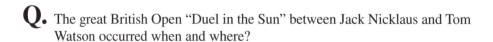

Q. The great British Open "Duel in the Sun" between Jack Nicklaus and Tom Watson occurred when and where?

A. In 1977, at Turnberry. Watson won.

Q. Two-time U.S. Open champion Andy North's only other PGA Tour victory came in what event?

A. The 1977 American Express-Westchester Classic.

———— ✸ ————

Q. What twosome captured the first Legends of Golf tournament in 1978?

A. Sam Snead and Gardner Dickinson.

———— ✸ ————

Q. Who was the first golfer to go as low as 63 in a British Open round?

A. Mark Hayes, who shot a 63 in the second round of the 1977 Open at Turnberry.

———— ✸ ————

Q. Gibby Gilbert was disqualified at the 1973 Atlanta Classic when he refused to sign his scorecard after suffering what kind of shortage at the eighteenth hole?

A. He ran out of golf balls and couldn't complete his round.

———— ✸ ————

Q. What two-time U.S. Women's Open champion won five U.S. Women's Amateurs before she turned pro, at age thirty-one, in 1970?

A. JoAnne (Gunderson) Carner.

———— ✸ ————

Q. What golfer won three consecutive PGA Tour events in 1978?

A. Gary Player, whose winning streak that year included the Masters.

———— ✸ ————

Q. What college freshman won the 1975 men's NCAA title?

A. Curtis Strange, of Wake Forest.

Ten 1970s Majors Whose Winners Weren't Exactly Household Names

1970 LPGA Championship—Shirley Englehorn
1971 Masters—Charles Coody
1972 LPGA Championship—Kathy Ahern
1973 Masters—Tommy Aaron
1974 PGA Seniors'—Roberto De Vicenzo
1975 U.S. Open—Lou Graham
1976 U.S. Open—Jerry Pate
1977 LPGA Championship—Chako Higuchi
1978 PGA Championship—John Mahaffey
1979 PGA Championship—David Graham

Q. In what year was Ryder Cup participation broadened to include all of Europe?

A. 1979.

Q. Under what circumstances did a "Sandra" win ten LPGA events in 1974, although JoAnne Carner tied for most victories that year with six?

A. Sandra Haynie (six victories), Sandra Palmer (two), Sandra Post (one), and Sandra Spuzich (one), to equal ten among them.

Q. What golfer won the most LPGA events during the seventies?

A. Kathy Whitworth, with twenty-eight victories.

Q. After turning pro, what future Masters champion's first tournament win was the 1973 San Antonio Texas Open?

A. Ben Crenshaw.

Q. Al Geiberger recorded the PGA Tour's first sub-60 round at what 1977 event?

A. "Mr. 59" earned his stripes at the Danny Thomas Memphis Classic.

Q. What tournament did Hale Irwin win twice as his only tour victories before winning his first U.S. Open title, in 1974?

A. The Heritage Classic, in 1971 and 1973.

Q. Future PGA Tour players Andy Bean and Gary Koch led what school to the 1973 NCAA golf title?

A. University of Florida.

Q. Whose victory in the 1975 Greater Milwaukee Open made him the most recent golfer over the age of fifty to win a regular PGA Tour event?

A. Art Wall Jr.

Q. In what year did a PGA Tour golfer for the first time ever win the Tour's first three events of the season?

A. 1974, courtesy of Johnny Miller.

Q. In 1978 little-known Bob Impaglia became the first man to suffer what indignity in a U.S. Open?

A. Penalized for slow play.

Q. What was the first PGA Tour event to award $100,000 as the winner's share?

A. The 1973 World Open Golf Championship, won by Miller Barber.

Earlier we saw Nancy Lopez swinging for the fences. This time it's **Johnny Miller**, at the 1978 Masters, going for broke. Note the bend in his left foot. That hurts! Golf's mod man of the disco era won a U.S. Open and a British Open, but could never quite get the hang of Augusta, where his best finish was second—three times.

(©PHIL SHELDON)

Q. Golfers with the last name of Miller won a total of nine PGA Tour events in 1974, with Johnny Miller winning eight and what other Miller winning one?

A. Allen Miller, whose victory that year at the Tallahassee Open was simultaneous with Johnny Miller's victory in the Tournament of Champions.

Q. Whose three-putt on the seventy-second hole at the 1970 British Open ultimately cost him the title?

A. Doug Sanders, who subsequently lost a play-off to Jack Nicklaus.

Q. Tom Watson earned a bachelor of arts degree in what major upon graduation from Stanford in 1971?

A. Psychology.

Q. What four-time winner of the U.S. Women's Open retired from competition in 1975 and became the LPGA's tournament director?

A. Betsy Rawls.

Q. In the 1970 U.S. Open, what fellow Texan and 1970 NCAA champion tied Ben Crenshaw for low amateur?

A. John Mahaffey.

Q. During his playing days at Wake Forest in the early seventies, what was Curtis Strange's nickname?

A. Brutus.

Q. What winner of a U.S. Open during the seventies came back from being eleven shots out of the lead at the halfway point?

A. Lou Graham, in 1975.

SCORECARD

9

60 Questions
Par: 4

Correct answers	Score	
58–60	Eagle	2
45–57	Birdie	3
30–44	Par	4
20–29	Bogey	5
10–19	Double Bogey	6
Less than 10	Triple Bogey	7

Your score _____

The
BACK
nine

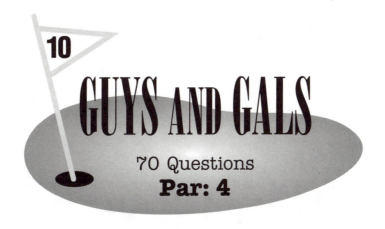

Q. Who was Nancy Lopez's first husband?

A. Tim Melton, a Houston sportscaster.

Q. Who is "Mr. X"?

A. Limelight-shy Miller Barber.

Q. First lady Hillary Rodham Clinton surprised her husband, President Bill Clinton, with a forty-ninth birthday gift consisting of a round of golf with what golfing great, one of the prez's all-time favorites?

A. Johnny Miller.

Q. What six-foot-tall blonde actress-singer and star of the 1980 film *Goldengirl* took up golf in her forties, was shooting in the 80s within four years, and has been a contributing writer for *Golf and Travel*?

A. Susan Anton.

Q. What TV tabloid-talk-show host, married to Connie Chung, is an excellent golfer as well?

A. Maury Povich.

Q. What relative newcomer to the LPGA was once one of Tiger Woods's *rumored* romantic interests?

A. Kelli Kuehne.

⎯⎯⎯ ∞∞∞ ⎯⎯⎯

Q. A veritable slowhand when it comes to strumming a guitar, what original officer of the recently formed Tournament Players Association has a brother and sister playing pro golf?

A. Larry Rinker, who sometimes joins rock groups while on the road, such as the Sons of the Beaches during Colonial week in Fort Worth.

⎯⎯⎯ ∞∞∞ ⎯⎯⎯

Q. Bing Crosby and Bob Hope both competed in what major amateur golf event?

A. The British Amateur.

⎯⎯⎯ ∞∞∞ ⎯⎯⎯

Q. Former ABC-TV golf producer Terry Jastrow is married to what actress?

A. Anne Archer.

⎯⎯⎯ ∞∞∞ ⎯⎯⎯

Q. "Dr. Dirt" is the oft-used nickname for what PGA Tour veteran who has a younger golfing brother named Bart?

A. Brad Bryant.

⎯⎯⎯ ∞∞∞ ⎯⎯⎯

Q. LPGA golfers Vickie Goetze-Ackerman and Annika Sorenstam, fierce amateur and collegiate rivals during the early 1990s, share what important date in their personal histories?

A. Both were married on January 4, 1997.

⎯⎯⎯ ∞∞∞ ⎯⎯⎯

Q. Who was Nick Faldo's caddie for most of the 1990s?

A. Fanny Sunneson.

Eighteen Sets of Golfers Who Have, for One Reason or Another, Been Mistaken for Each Other

Ken Brown, Ken Green	Craig Parry, Chris Perry
Jan Stephenson, Laura Baugh	Jack Fleck, Jim Flick
Mark McCumber, Mark O'Meara	Tim Simpson, Scott Simpson
Stuart Appleby, Robert Allenby	Sandra Palmer, Sandra Post
David Peoples, Peter Persons	Nick Faldo, Nick Price
Dillard Pruitt, Andy Dillard	Jack Nicklaus, Jack Nicholson
Brad Faxon, Brad Fabel	Bruce Crampton, Bruce Devlin
Gary Koch, Scott Hoch	Tommy Aaron, Frank Beard
Bill Rogers, Joel Edwards	Larry Hinson, Johnny Miller

Q. What PGA Tour veteran is married to his mother's brother's wife's sister's daughter?

A. David Edwards (wife Jonnie).

—⊶∞⊷—

Q. What network TV morning show cohost married in 1998 and promptly cleaned out his coveted golf closet to create much-needed wardrobe space?

A. Matt Lauer.

—⊶∞⊷—

Q. What winner of all three American majors once managed an all-female rock band, the Ladybirds?

A. Raymond Floyd.

—⊶∞⊷—

Q. What ex-wife of a former Masters champion was herself a crack tennis and polo player?

A. Deborah Couples, Fred's ex.

Q. "The Boss of the Moss" is the nickname of what multiple-tournament winner of the nineties?

A. Loren Roberts.

———

Q. Golfer Pat Bradley's brother, Chris Bradley, proposed to what LPGA golfer via electronic scoreboard at a Boston Red Sox game at Fenway Park?

A. Melissa McNamara.

———

Q. What leggy American golfer grabbed almost as much attention at the 1996 U.S. Women's Open for her navy blue knit minidress as for her runner-up finish to Annika Sorenstam?

A. Kris Tschetter.

———

Q. Justin Leonard, the 1997 British Open champion, for a while in 1993–1994 dated the daughter of what former PGA Championship winner and U.S. Ryder Cup captain?

A. Lanny Wadkins (father of Jessica).

———

Q. What brother-and-sister combo won the mixed-team JCPenney Classic in 1985?

A. Larry and Laurie Rinker.

———

Q. What veteran golfer has a spouse and a sister who have played on the LPGA tour, a brother who played the PGA Tour, and a father who is a PGA professional?

A. Jim Gallagher Jr.

———

Q. Steve Ellis, a former editor at *Golfweek*, was married to what LPGA golfer until their divorce in 1995?

A. Tammie Green.

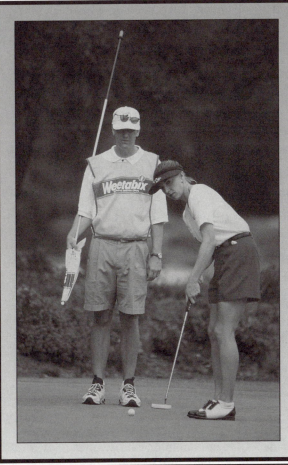

Throughout the 1990s **Kris Tschetter** has been one of the LPGA's most fashionable players, as well as one of its most promising in terms of play. She was runner-up to Annika Sorenstam in the 1996 U.S. Women's Open, although she entered the 1999 LPGA season with only two victories to her credit, and one of those was the 1991 JCPenney Classic, an unofficial tour event, with partner Billy Andrade. Here she is competing in the 1997 Weetabix British Women's Open.

(JAN TRAYLEN PHOTO/ ©PHIL SHELDON)

Q. What singing superstar of *Titanic* fame has been a prominent pitch person for Callaway?

A. Celine Dion.

Q. Who was Champagne Tony?

A. Tony Lema, the 1964 British Open champion who was killed in a 1966 plane crash near Chicago.

Q. Former Masters champion Bob Goalby is an uncle to what PGA Tour pro who has contended at several Masters Tournaments and has been a Ryder Cup participant?

A. Jay Haas.

Q. What PGA Tour golfer was married on the eighteenth green at the TPC at Las Colinas, site of the Byron Nelson Classic, just prior to that event in 1994?

A. Billy Mayfair, to Tammy McIntyre.

Q. What is Gil Morgan's full first name?

A. Gilmer.

Q. What single-digit handicapper was allowed to pair with his wife, Annika Sorenstam, at the 1998 JCPenney Classic?

A. David Esch.

Q. What former U.S. Women's Open champion and winner of two other women's majors posed nude in a bathtub full of golf balls for a calendar?

A. Jan Stephenson.

Q. Which of *Charlie's Angels* took up golf in the 1990s and signed an endorsement deal for a golf-equipment manufacturer?

A. Cheryl Ladd (who played Kris Monroe in *Charlie's Angels*).

Q. Laura Norman and Julie Crenshaw had what occupation in common before they married their golfing husbands, Greg and Ben?

A. They were flight attendants.

Ten Photogenic LPGA Tournament Winners Who Have Also Posed in *Fairway* Magazine's Annual Fashion Issue

1. Cindy Flom
2. Kris Tschetter
3. Barb Bunkowsky-Scherbak
4. Dale Eggeling
5. Cindy Figg-Currier
6. Chris Johnson
7. Nancy Lopez
8. Cindy Mackey
9. Nancy Scranton
10. Sherri Steinhauer

Q. Who is "Big Momma"?

A. LPGA Hall of Famer JoAnne Carner.

Q. David Ogrin took time out from the middle of the 1986 Vantage Championship in San Antonio for what event?

A. His wedding to Sharon Edwards.

Q. The son of what golfing great married a dancer who landed gigs on MTV's Music Awards and a Madonna tour, among other things?

A. Jack Nicklaus, whose son Gary, a PGA Tour rookie, gained an appreciation for a different kind of athleticism through his now ex-wife, Jill.

Q. What blond-maned yet oft-injured golfer, while still a bachelor, admitted he fibbed in the PGA Tour media guide by listing cool-sounding hobbies like surfing to impress the babes?

A. Bill Glasson, who said he later learned the only thing groupies cared about was a golfer's position on the money list.

Q. What American woman left the LPGA to play in Japan in 1992, returned to the States for a while, then left for several years in France after marrying a Frenchman?

A. Patti Rizzo.

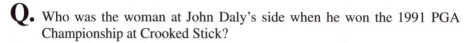

Q. Who was the woman at John Daly's side when he won the 1991 PGA Championship at Crooked Stick?

A. Bettye Fulford, who became his second wife.

Q. What chic six-footer and LPGA veteran has been known more for her leather boots with golf spikes, one-piece bodysuits, cheetah-print leotards, and other gaudy apparel than for her golf game?

A. Deborah Vidal (formerly Deborah McHaffie).

Q. What Senior Tour golfer and former U.S. Open champion served in the President's Honor Guard while enlisted in the army?

A. Lou Graham.

Q. Former NFL placekicker Goran Longmerth married what LPGA golfer in 1993?

A. Heather Farr.

Q. Once asked what she thought about golf, what royal lady said, "I prefer to take the dog out"?

A. Princess Anne, of Great Britain.

Q. Actress Kirstie Alley is a cousin of what tour golfer?

A. Bruce Lietzke.

Miss Teen Golfer U.S.A.

Laura Baugh was just sixteen years old when she won the 1971 U.S. Women's Amateur Championship, the same year she was named the *L.A. Times*'s Woman of the Year. A year later *Golf Digest* tabbed her as the Most Beautiful Golfer. Blonde, beautiful, and with a game full of birdies, Baugh appeared a shoo-in as the LPGA's superstar-to-be of the 1970s and 1980s. Counting endorsement dollars, Baugh might have been the LPGA's leading money winner for most of the 1970s, even though she never won a tournament in that time. In fact, Baugh was still winless through the 1998 season. A recovering alcoholic, she is mom to seven children she has raised against the backdrop of a shaky golf career and an on-again, off-again marriage to fellow pro golfer Bobby Cole.

It appears that **Laura Baugh** is doing more for the sale of bell bottoms here than she is for her score, tracking a putt that, judging from her facial expression, doesn't seem to have much promise.

(©PHIL SHELDON)

Q. Who was Nick Faldo's longtime girlfriend in the 1990s (a relationship that broke up his marriage)?

A. Brenna Cepelak, who had played golf at the University of Arizona.

Q. What winner of the 2000 Players Championship is discreetly nicknamed "Halimony" by his peers?

A. Hal Sutton, who has been married several times.

Q. The LPGA in 1968 officially sanctioned what type of apparel for tournament play?

A. Miniskirts.

Q. A 1993 rumor apparently ignited by a British tabloid had what LPGA star divorcing so she could marry Fred Couples?

A. Dottie Mochrie (now Dottie Pepper), who did indeed divorce several years later, although it wasn't to marry Fred.

Q. Charging that he allegedly stole money owed to her in their divorce settlement, Jan Stephenson sued whom in 1994?

A. Eddie Vossler.

Q. Phil Mickelson's wife, the former Amy McBride, was a cheerleader for what professional sports team?

A. The NBA's Phoenix Suns.

Q. What is LPGA player Caroline McMillan's maiden name?

A. Caroline Pierce.

Here we see **Nick Faldo** in one of his happier times, yukking it up under a wig while two of the women in his life look on. Longtime Faldo caddie Fanny Sunneson is on the left, and former Faldo squeeze Brenna Cepelak is on the right. Normally stone stoic Hogan-like when it comes to golf, Faldo here lets his hair down. This is something Ben Hogan never would have done. The occasion here is Faldo's caddying for rock singer Huey Lewis at the 1996 Pebble Beach National Pro-Am. (©PHIL SHELDON)

Q. *Cosmopolitan* magazine in 1996 included what golfer as one of its twenty-five most eligible bachelors in the world?

A. Justin Leonard.

Q. Who was "Lighthorse Harry"?

A. Tour pro Harry Cooper, who won more than two dozen events as one of the winningest players never to have won a major.

Q. A young woman by the name of Elizabeth Doll won what USGA national championship in 1967?

A. The U.S. Junior Girls. Doll later was one of Hollis Stacy's sorority sisters at Rollins College, then married to become Elizabeth Story, and eventually quit golf.

Q. What was the maiden name of Judy Dickinson, whose late husband Gardner Dickinson had been her teacher?

A. Judy Clark.

———— ∞ ————

Q. What sibling of LPGA veteran Cathy Gerring has also been a tour golfer?

A. Her brother Bill Kratzert, once a promising golfer on the PGA Tour in the early eighties.

———— ∞ ————

Q. The initials in golfer D. A. Weibring's name stand for what?

A. Donald Albert, although Weibring jokingly says they mean "Don't Ask."

———— ∞ ————

Q. What U.S. Open champion of the eighties has a twin brother who has also played some pro golf?

A. Curtis Strange, whose twin brother is Allen.

———— ∞ ————

Q. Fred Couples remarried in 1998 to whom?

A. Thais Bren.

———— ∞ ————

Q. What girlfriend/caddie of 1996 U.S. Amateur runner-up Steve Scott was a decent collegiate golfer and even landed a golf-equipment endorsement deal?

A. Kristi Hommel, who replaced Michelle McGann on the payroll at (doomed) Lynx.

———— ∞ ————

Q. The husband of TV golf commentator Judy Rankin has what name that sounds like an exclamation of victory, yet has negative connotations for folks with balky putters?

A. Yippy.

Ten Tournament Winners with Cool, Catchy, or Comical Names

Name	Last Pre-1999 Tour Victory
George Burns	1987 S. L. Bros.-Andy Williams Open
Fred Funk	1998 Southern Farm Bureau Classic
Scott Gump	1994 Nike Greater Greenville Classic
Robin Hood	1989 Planters Pat Bradley International
Rocco Mediate	1993 Kmart Greater Greensboro Open
Jodie Mudd	1990 Nabisco Championships
Pearl Sinn	1998 State Farm Rail Classic
Lance Ten Broeck	1984 Magnolia State Classic
Jim Thorpe	1986 Seiko Tucson Match Play
Duffy Waldorf	1995 LaCantera Texas Open

Q. The gift of a pineapple given by Phoenix businessman Trent Whitehead to pro golfer Barb Thomas on their first date, a 1995 Super Bowl-watching party at her place, foreshadowed what event?

A. Barb's winning her first pro event, the LPGA's Cup Noodles Hawaiian Open, ending a twelve-year drought. The two were married weeks later.

———&&&———

Q. Todd Haller caddied for and was engaged to what LPGA star before they broke up in 1996?

A. Karrie Webb.

———&&&———

Q. What kind of implement did Brenna Cepelak use to inflict damage on Nick Faldo's Porsche during their 1998 breakup?

A. A nine-iron.

———&&&———

Q. What is Duffy Waldorf's real first name?

A. James.

Strange but True

This book's author grew up in the sixties and seventies playing golf at tiny Richford (Vermont) Country Club, where the two women running the clubhouse snack bar and golf shop, Betty and Buddy, were wives of two longtime members. Their last names were, respectively, Esty and Lauder.

Q. In December 1998 what did a young woman by the name of Joanna Jagoda do to catch the eye of the world's golf media?

A. She accompanied bachelor Tiger Woods to the Presidents Cup competition in Australia.

Q. What is the first name of European superstar Colin Montgomerie's wife, in which the vowels outnumber the consonants?

A. Eimear.

Q. The brother of what LPGA Hall of Famer was the medalist at the 1998 U.S. Mid-Amateur?

A. Patty Sheehan, whose brother, Steve Sheehan, claims to be the better skier of the two siblings in one of Vermont's most notable skiing families.

Q. Who was John Daly's first wife?
A. Dale Crafton.

Q. What is Tiger Woods's given first name?
A. Eldrick.

Q. Who is the trick-shot artist with a canine companion named Benji Hogan?
A. Dennis Walters.

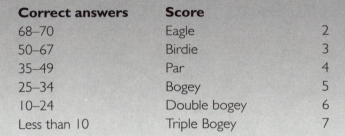

SCORECARD

70 Questions
Par: 4

Correct answers	Score	
68–70	Eagle	2
50–67	Birdie	3
35–49	Par	4
25–34	Bogey	5
10–24	Double bogey	6
Less than 10	Triple Bogey	7

Your score _____

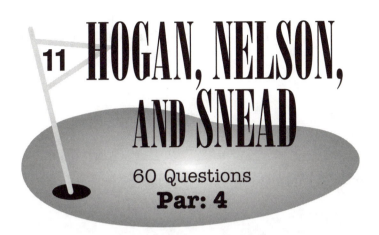

11 HOGAN, NELSON, AND SNEAD

60 Questions
Par: 4

Q. What golfer better known for his record as an amateur than as a pro ended Byron Nelson's streak of eleven consecutive victories in 1945?

A. Freddie Haas, at the Memphis Open.

Q. In what Texas town was Ben Hogan born?

A. Stephenville (not Dublin as long reported).

Q. Nelson and Hogan caddied together at what Fort Worth golf club as youngsters?

A. Glen Garden.

Q. How did Sam Snead fare in his first U.S. Open try, in 1937?

A. He finished second in an event he would never win.

Q. What rare scoring feat did Snead achieve in 1959 at the Sam Snead Festival?

A. He shot a 59.

Q. Byron Nelson's final U.S. tour victory came in what event?

A. The 1951 Crosby.

Q. Ben Hogan's first official tour victory was actually a two-man triumph with what other golfer in the 1938 Hershey (Pennsylvania) Four-Ball?

A. Vic Ghezzi.

Q. What is Sam Snead's middle name?

A. Jackson, for Civil War general Stonewall Jackson.

Q. What winner of the 1938 Masters and the 1939 PGA Championship was considered by Ben Hogan to be one of his best friends, as evidenced by Hogan's dedication of his book *Power Golf* to him?

A. Henry Picard.

Q. Needing only a par at the last hole to win the 1939 U.S. Open, Sam Snead did what instead?

A. He triple-bogied and lost.

Q. In how many majors did various combinations of Hogan, Nelson, and Snead finish one-two?

A. Four: 1940 PGA, Nelson over Snead; 1942 Masters, Nelson over Hogan; 1953 U.S. Open, Hogan over Snead; and 1954 Masters, Snead over Hogan.

Q. Sam Snead's first victory in a major came in what event?

A. The 1942 PGA Championship.

Q. Ben Hogan's first individual victory as a professional came in what event?

A. The 1940 North and South Open, at Pinehurst No. 2.

If **Ben Hogan** wasn't the greatest golfer of the twentieth century, at least he was the most enigmatic.

(COURTESY OF LIBRARY OF CONGRESS)

Q. Which of these three golfers held the record for most tour victories before the age of thirty, eventually broken by Jack Nicklaus?

A. Sam Snead, with twenty-seven (Nicklaus had twenty-nine).

Q. As a young pro Sam Snead apprenticed under head pro Freddy Gleim at what Virginia golf club?

A. Homestead.

Q. In what year did Ben Hogan found the Hogan Company?

A. 1953.

Q. How many total victories did Byron Nelson end up with in 1945, the year he won eleven straight?

A. Eighteen.

Q. With what equipment manufacturer has Sam Snead been associated since 1937?

A. Wilson.

Q. What actor portrayed Ben Hogan (as an adult) in the biopic *Follow the Sun*?

A. Glenn Ford.

Q. Sam Snead's missed putt of two and a half feet on the eighteenth hole of a play-off at the 1949 U.S. Open allowed what golfer to win?

A. Lew Worsham.

Q. Snead, Hogan, and Nelson were born within what time span?

A. Seven months, in 1912.

Q. Nelson started his incredible streak of eleven consecutive victories in 1945 by teaming with what pal to win the Miami Four-Ball?

A. Jug McSpaden.

Q. What club did Ben Hogan actually hit to the eighteenth green in the last round at Merion en route to his 1950 U.S. Open comeback victory?

A. One-iron, although one of his books mistakenly said it was a two-iron.

Q. In 1933, right about the time Hogan, Snead, and Nelson were breaking into the pro ranks, the golf tour stopped in what ominously named coal-mining town in Kentucky?

A. Hazard (and, no, Ben, Sam, and Byron were not "the dukes of Hazard").

Q. Who was the firstborn of the three?

A. Byron Nelson, born on February 4, 1912.

Q. Sam Snead was undefeated in Ryder Cup play until he lost a singles match to what golfer in the 1953 competition?

A. Harry Weetman.

Q. Who authored the book *My Partner, Ben Hogan*?

A. Fellow golfer Jimmy Demaret.

Q. After Sam Snead married his wife, Audrey, they honeymooned at what popular tourist attraction, just a couple of hours away from a tournament that Snead won that same week?

A. Niagara Falls.

Q. The first time the Hogan Company was sold (1960), it was bought by whom?

A. AMF (American Machine and Foundry).

Q. Sam Snead's first endorsement contract, in 1936, was with what equipment manufacturer that paid him $500 a month, gave him a new set of clubs, and provided him with a dozen balls a month?

A. Dunlop.

Sam Snead's Ten Tips for Success at Match Play

1. Play more conservatively early in the match.
2. When in doubt, check your opponent's lie.
3. After winning a hole, concentrate on hitting a solid drive.
4. When the momentum is going against you, change the pace of the match.
5. Always figure your opponent will make (a long putt).
6. Never give up on yourself.
7. Don't get mad, get even.
8. When you decide to gamble, "Katy bar the door."
9. Know the rule differences for match play.
10. Always keep the pressure on your opponent.

(SOURCE: *Pigeons, Marks, and Hustlers,*
BY SAM SNEAD AND JERRY TARDE AS ADAPTED FOR *Golf Digest*)

Q. What fellow pro and longtime traveling companion of Snead's during the 1930s was a Quaker?

A. Johnny Bulla.

Q. Byron Nelson was paid $500 in 1936 to endorse what kind of product that he actually disdained?

A. Cigarettes (a brand called 20 Grand). Nelson later failed in an attempt to cancel the six-month contract.

Q. Sam Snead beat Ben Hogan in a play-off at what 1950 tournament that marked Hogan's first appearance since nearly being killed in a 1949 automobile mishap?

A. The L.A. Open.

Q. Who was the youngest of these three?

A. Ben Hogan, born on August 13, 1912.

Sam Snead has been one of golf's most dashing figures for decades.

(© PHIL SHELDON)

Q. Nelson's first wife, who passed away in 1985, had what first name?

A. Louise.

Q. In Ben Hogan's near-fatal crash on February 2, 1949, what collided with his car?

A. A Greyhound bus.

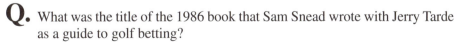

Q. What was the title of the 1986 book that Sam Snead wrote with Jerry Tarde as a guide to golf betting?

A. *Pigeons, Marks, and Hustlers.*

Q. How old was Snead when, in the same year, he finished third behind Lee Trevino and Jack Nicklaus in the PGA Championship and placed second in the Los Angeles Open?

A. Sixty-two, in 1974.

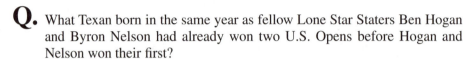

Q. What Texan born in the same year as fellow Lone Star Staters Ben Hogan and Byron Nelson had already won two U.S. Opens before Hogan and Nelson won their first?

A. Ralph Guldahl.

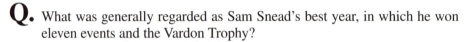

Q. What was generally regarded as Sam Snead's best year, in which he won eleven events and the Vardon Trophy?

A. 1950, although Ben Hogan won that season's Player of the Year Award on the strength of popular sentiment for his comeback from the auto accident.

Q. To what rank was Ben Hogan ultimately promoted while serving in the U.S. Army Air Corps during World War II?

A. Captain.

Q. Sam Snead won what tour event eight times, a record number for a golfer winning the same event?

A. Greater Greensboro Open.

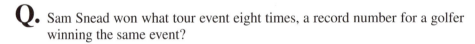

Q. Why was Byron Nelson rejected for military service during World War II?

A. He was what in those days was called "a free bleeder."

Q. What was the only year in the ten-year period between 1945 and 1954 in which neither Nelson, Snead, nor Hogan won a major?

A. 1947.

Q. In his great year of 1953, Hogan won five out of how many tournaments that he entered?

A. Six.

———— ✺ ————

Q. Hogan gave what name to his fantasy playmate, who "motivated" Ben to be the hardest worker at everything he did?

A. Hennie Bogan.

———— ✺ ————

Q. What is Sam Snead's relationship to fellow pro golfer J. C. Snead?

A. Sam is J. C.'s uncle.

———— ✺ ————

Q. As a publicity gimmick in 1942, Byron Nelson played right field for what minor league baseball team?

A. Toledo Mudhens.

———— ✺ ————

Q. Sam Snead reportedly settled for $2 million what kind of lawsuit brought against him in 1992?

A. For damages resulting from an auto accident in Augusta, Georgia, during the week of the Masters Tournament.

———— ✺ ————

Q. Ben Hogan's last tournament appearance came in what 1971 event, which he failed to finish?

A. Houston Champions International.

———— ✺ ————

Q. Years after having played golf with Sam Snead on a number of occasions, former president Richard Nixon told Snead that the most memorable feat he had seen Snead perform on a golf course was what?

A. Throwing a rock that killed a snake lying on a rock in a creek.

Swing, Byron

Most great golfers can remember back to when they came to a fork in the road presenting a choice between trying to chase a white ball for a living, or living out a childhood dream that might have included visions of becoming, say, a fireman or a seamstress. **Byron Nelson**'s moment of enlightenment apparently came when he was fifteen years old and was among the spectators watching Walter Hagen win his fifth PGA Championship. That was in 1927, at Cedar Crest in Dallas. A promising baseball player as well, Nelson was enraptured by what he saw, coming away ready to give golf a serious fling.

Q. On what course did Ben Hogan win the only British Open in which he competed, in 1953?

A. Carnoustie.

Q. What Fort Worth businessman and golf lover was Ben Hogan's longtime confidante, mentor, and financial backer?

A. Marvin Leonard.

Q. With what baseball hitting star did Sam Snead participate in a 1960 *Golf Digest* story in which each man analyzed the other's swing?

A. Ted Williams.

Q. On what venue did Ben Hogan win the first of his four (official) U.S. Open titles?

A. L.A.'s Riviera.

Q. With what LPGA player did the normally reclusive Hogan strike up a good friendship in the 1980s and 1990s, occasionally joining her to hit shag balls and help her with her swing?

A. Kris Tschetter.

Byron Nelson retired from full-time competitive golf while in his mid-thirties to spend more time at the Texas ranch he and his wife Louise bought with his winnings.

(PHOTO REPRINTED BY PERMISSION OF BYRON NELSON FROM HIS AUTOBIOGRAPHY, *How I Played The Game.*)

Q. Byron Nelson nearly died from what childhood illness at age eleven?

A. Typhoid fever.

Q. What magazine paid Ben Hogan $10,000 in 1954 to write an article about his so-called Secret?

A. *Life*.

Q. Byron Nelson won what European national championship in 1955, four years after he had won what turned out to be his last U.S. tour title?

A. French Open.

Q. Unhappy with the first batch of clubs manufactured by his company, Ben Hogan did what?

A. He trashed the clubs and started over from scratch, at an estimated cost of $100,000.

11

SCORECARD

60 Questions
Par: 4

Correct answers	Score	
58–60	Eagle	2
45–57	Birdie	3
30–44	Par	4
20–29	Bogey	5
10–19	Double Bogey	6
Less than 10	Triple Bogey	7

Your score _____

12

THE EIGHTIES

60 Questions
Par: 4

Q. What Kansas City native won an Open by a nine-shot margin during this decade?

A. Amy Alcott, the 1980 U.S. Women's Open champ.

Q. What Texan won the 1981 British Open and was one of the world's hottest golfers around that time, although within three years he was a common object of the preposition in "Whatever happened to—"?

A. Bill Rogers.

Q. What prominent nonwinner of the Masters not enamored of Augusta National opened the 1989 Masters with a 67 that made him, at forty-nine, the oldest man ever to lead the event?

A. Lee Trevino.

Q. Who was the first Senior PGA Tour golfer over the age of sixty to win a senior event?

A. Roberto De Vicenzo, at sixty-one, winner of the 1984 Merrill Lynch Commemorative.

Q. What two dominant male players of the eighties were born only eleven days apart?

A. Greg Norman and Curtis Strange.

Q. Laura Davies defeated what two players in an eighteen-hole play-off to capture the 1987 U.S. Women's Open?

A. Ayako Okamato and JoAnne Carner.

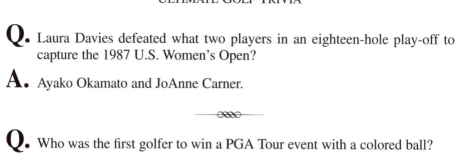

Q. Who was the first golfer to win a PGA Tour event with a colored ball?

A. Wayne Levi, whose lucky color at the 1982 Hawaiian Open was orange.

Q. What two Senior PGA Tour golfers each successfully defended his 1984 major-tournament title in 1985?

A. Miller Barber in the Senior Open and Arnold Palmer in the Senior Players Championship.

Q. In what year was the all-exempt PGA Tour instituted, to include a new category of the top 125 money winners from the previous year?

A. 1983.

Q. Who was the only man to win the Masters more than once during the eighties?

A. Seve Ballesteros, who won in 1980 and 1983.

Q. While tinkering with his fleet of vintage automobiles, what former U.S. Amateur and U.S. Open champ broke his arm in 1984?

A. Gene Littler.

Q. What winner of three PGA Tour events during the late eighties and Fred Couples's former roommate at the University of Houston has putted lefty much of his career even though he hits all his other shots right-handed?

A. Blaine McCallister.

Q. The 1980 Walt Disney World National Team Championship went to what two brothers?

A. Danny and David Edwards.

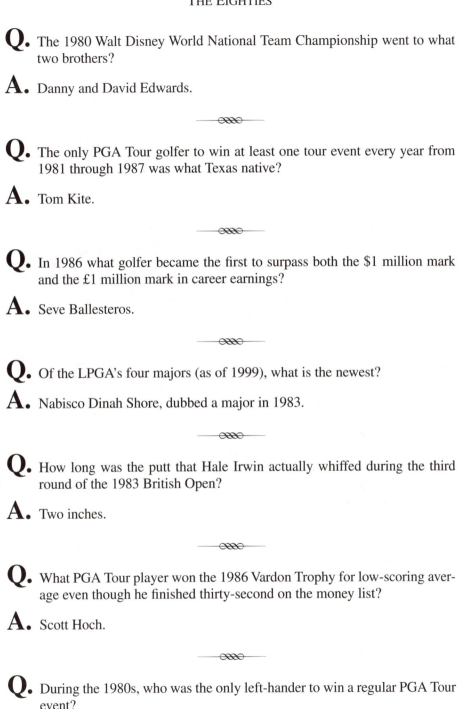

Q. The only PGA Tour golfer to win at least one tour event every year from 1981 through 1987 was what Texas native?

A. Tom Kite.

Q. In 1986 what golfer became the first to surpass both the $1 million mark and the £1 million mark in career earnings?

A. Seve Ballesteros.

Q. Of the LPGA's four majors (as of 1999), what is the newest?

A. Nabisco Dinah Shore, dubbed a major in 1983.

Q. How long was the putt that Hale Irwin actually whiffed during the third round of the 1983 British Open?

A. Two inches.

Q. What PGA Tour player won the 1986 Vardon Trophy for low-scoring average even though he finished thirty-second on the money list?

A. Scott Hoch.

Q. During the 1980s, who was the only left-hander to win a regular PGA Tour event?

A. Ernie Gonzalez, at the 1986 Pensacola Open.

Q. Pat Bradley won three of the LPGA majors in 1986 and fared how well in the fourth, the U.S. Women's Open?

A. She finished fifth, narrowly missing a Grand Slam.

Pat Bradley

(COURTESY OF LPGA)

Q. By the time Tiger Woods turned pro in 1996, who had been the last African American to make it out of Q-School and onto the PGA Tour?

A. Adrian Stills, from the 1985 Q-School. Woods, by the way, has never had to go through the Q-School meat grinder.

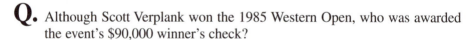

Q. Although Scott Verplank won the 1985 Western Open, who was awarded the event's $90,000 winner's check?

A. Runner-up Jim Thorpe. Verplank was still playing as an amateur.

Q. In what year did Tom Watson win his fifth British Open title?

A. 1983.

Q. In how many majors had Ben Crenshaw finished second before he won his first, the 1984 Masters?

A. Five, including two in 1979—the British Open and the PGA Championship.

Q. Strangely, what was Curtis Strange's highest rank in the World Rankings, even after he had won the 1987 World Series of Golf; the 1988 Memorial, U.S. Open, and Tour Championship; and the Open again in 1989?

A. Fourth.

Q. Whose unlikely four-victory season of 1984 might have included five wins had he not been penalized two strokes at the U.S. Open, where he missed getting into a play-off by one shot?

A. Denis Watson, whose punishment was meted out for his waiting too long for a hanging putt to drop.

Q. Alice Miller practically dominated LPGA play in the first half of 1985, winning four events while quickly breaking the single-season money record, although what golfer had an even stronger second half that year to finish one up on Miller with five victories and the number one spot on the money list?

A. Nancy Lopez.

Q. Why did Nancy Lopez suddenly disappear from the leader board in 1986?

A. She was pregnant and then gave birth to daughter Erinn Shea.

Q. What TV football commentator and former NFL quarterback came out of the NBC booth in the mid-1980s to make a successful bid to play on the Senior PGA Tour?

A. John Brodie.

Q. What PGA Tour golfer won his fifth Vardon Trophy in 1980?

A. Lee Trevino.

Fast Ford

Doug Ford, the 1957 Masters Tournament winner, has received his share of criticism in recent years for continuing to exercise his lifetime Masters exemption decades well past the time when he could realistically entertain thoughts of contending, let alone winning. That aside, give Ford a thumbs-up for one virtue in particular—he plays fast. No dawdling for him—this Ford motors. His reputation for quickness in getting around the course was cemented at the 1981 U.S. Senior Open at Oakland Hills, where for one of his rounds he was paired with the quick, or at least quick-tempered, Jim Ferree. Ferree had the honors when they arrived at one par-three hole, where he promptly hit his tee shot into a greenside bunker. Ferree's ball had barely stopped moving when Ford pushed peg into ground, teed his ball up, and took his stance. Ferree, meanwhile, had stormed back to his golf bag, where he slammed his club back inside and angrily yanked out his sand wedge. Out came the wedge—out of Ferree's bag and out of his hand. It catapulted across the tee and nailed Ford just as he was starting his swing. No problem. Ford kept right on with his swing, hardly looking up as he played away.

Q. In the eighties what two golfing buddies founded the CalGreen Foundation to help fund a home for abandoned and abused children?

A. Mark Calcavecchia and Ken Green. Calcavecchia later had his name removed from the project.

Q. Who was the first player to go as low as 61 in a Senior PGA Tour round?

A. Lee Elder, at the 1985 Commemorative.

Q. A freak waterskiing mishap in 1985 nearly killed what PGA Tour player?

A. Jim Nelford.

Q. The Symmetry Standard instituted in 1987 by the USGA outlawed what?

A. Golf balls that correct themselves in flight.

Q. What LPGA golfer won seven events during a thirteen-month span bridging 1986 and 1987, including a U.S. Women's Open and an LPGA Championship?

A. Jane Geddes.

Q. What quiet-spoken "journeyman" pro of the 1960s and 1970s became a Senior PGA Tour sensation in 1986 with two victories and a second-place finish in his first three events?

A. Dale Douglass.

Q. In 1980 what woman became the first LPGA golfer to win more than $200,000 in one season?

A. Beth Daniel.

Q. Dave Eichelberger won the 1980 Bay Hill Classic while wearing what kind of apparel to ward off the wind and cold?

A. Panty hose.

Q. Whose victory at the 1985 Hilton Head Senior Invitational made him the first Senior PGA Tour player over the age of sixty-one to win a senior event?

A. Mike Fetchick, who was sixty-three at the time.

Q. Calvin Peete led the PGA Tour in what major statistical category for ten consecutive years starting in 1981?

A. Driving accuracy.

Ten PGA Tour Winners from the 1980s Who Qualify for "Whatever Happened to . . . ?" Status

Jeff Mitchell, 1980 Phoenix Open
Bill Rogers, 1981 British Open
Jim Simons, 1982 Bing Crosby National Pro-Am
Mike Nicolette, 1983 Bay Hill Classic
Lance Ten Broeck, 1984 Magnolia State Classic
Woody Blackburn, 1985 Isuzu/Andy Williams San Diego Open
Fred Wadsworth, 1986 Southern Open Invitational
T. C. Chen, 1987 Los Angeles Open
Morris Hatalsky, 1988 Kemper Open
Jim Booros, 1989 Deposit Guaranty Classic

Q. Betsy King's first major victory of her career came in what event?

A. The 1987 Nabisco Dinah Shore.

Q. Payne Stewart briefly played what winter tour before qualifying for the U.S. PGA Tour in 1981?

A. The Asian Tour, where he finished third in the Order of Merit in early 1981.

Q. What colorful and outspoken golfer in the 1980s once referred to PGA Tour Commissioner Deane Beman as a thief?

A. Mac O'Grady, who said other things as well after Beman fined the petulant golfer for alleged verbal abuse of a tournament volunteer (which O'Grady flatly denied).

Q. What was the first regular PGA Tour event to offer a million-dollar purse?

A. The Panasonic Las Vegas Invitational, in 1983.

Q. The chip-in Larry Mize made on the second hole of a sudden-death play-off to win the 1987 Masters was how long?

A. 140 feet.

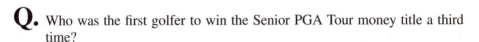

Q. Who was the first golfer to win the Senior PGA Tour money title a third time?

A. Don January, who finished number one in 1980, 1983, and 1984.

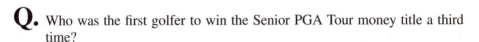

Q. Prior to Tiger Woods, who was the last golfer to win at least seven PGA tour events in one season?

A. Tom Watson, 1980.

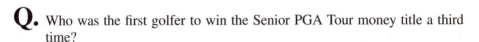

Q. What disabled veteran and Senior PGA Tour golfer protested the USGA's ban on carts at the 1987 U.S. Senior Open by using crutches before withdrawing after nine holes?

A. Charlie Owens.

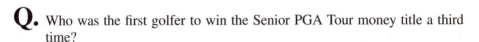

Q. What PGA Tour event in 1987 became the first to offer a $2 million purse?

A. The Nabisco Championships, later renamed the Tour Championship.

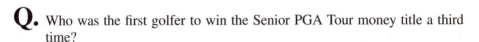

Q. What former Oklahoma State golfer had a career year in 1986, his second full PGA Tour season, with four victories, including a major?

A. Bob Tway, who holed out from the sand at the seventy-second hole of the PGA Championship to defeat Greg Norman.

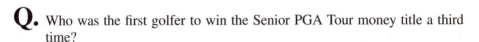

Q. A plaque at Westchester's par-five eighteenth commemorates the double eagle scored there by what winner of the 1982 Westchester Classic?

A. Bob Gilder.

Jan Stephenson's good looks and calendar poses often overshadowed her golf game, which happened to be among the best in the world for a number of years. Here she is in 1981 lining up a putt in the LPGA Championship, an event she won the following year.

(©PHIL SHELDON)

Q. What "pinup girl" of women's golf won majors in three consecutive years during the early 1980s?

A. Jan Stephenson, who won the 1981 Peter Jackson Classic, the 1982 LPGA Championship, and the 1983 U.S. Women's Open.

Q. T. C. Chen suffered what rare golf-swing calamity in the fourth round of the 1985 U.S. Open, which he subsequently lost by one stroke to Andy North?

A. Chen double-hit a chip shot and was assessed a two-stroke penalty.

Q. Who comprised the first female pairing ever invited to play in the Legends of Golf Tournament?

A. Mickey Wright and Kathy Whitworth, who tied for nineteenth out of twenty-eight teams at the 1985 event.

Q. Jerry Pate won the 1982 Tournament Players Championship at Sawgrass and then celebrated by playfully pushing what two men into the water beside the eighteenth green?

A. Tour commissioner Deane Beman and course architect Pete Dye.

Q. A 1987 *Golf Digest* survey of PGA Tour players identified what golfer as the fastest player on tour?

A. Lanny Wadkins.

Q. On what hole at which venue did Tom Watson chip in for a fourth-round birdie that effectively gave him the 1982 U.S. Open victory over Jack Nicklaus?

A. The seventeenth at Pebble Beach.

Q. What son of a famous entertainer won one of the most dramatic U.S. Amateurs ever contested, coming back from four holes down with ten remaining to win on the first extra hole in 1981?

A. Nathaniel Crosby, Bing's son.

Q. What two highly quotable golfers of the 1980s were involved in helping to organize a UCLA scientific study of the yips?

A. Mac O'Grady and Gary McCord.

Q. Who finished second to Jack Nicklaus when the Bear won the 1986 Masters at age forty-six?

A. Tom Kite and Greg Norman tied for the runner-up spot.

12

SCORECARD

60 Questions
Par: 4

Correct answers	Score	
58–60	Eagle	2
45–57	Birdie	3
30–44	Par	4
20–29	Bogey	5
10–19	Double bogey	6
Less than 10	Triple Bogey	7

Your score _____

13

THE ENTOURAGES

40 Questions
Par: 3

(CADDIES, AGENTS, TEACHERS, ETC.)

Q. Caddie Mike "Fluff" Cowan parted ways with what golfer in 1996 to take ownership of Tiger Woods's bag?

A. Peter Jacobsen.

Q. What founder of a prominent sports agency first gained notoriety as Arnold Palmer's manager?

A. Mark McCormack, who founded International Management Group (IMG).

Q. Bruce Lietzke's caddie once stuck what perishable into Lietzke's bag at the end of a season to test how long Lietzke would go in the off-season without touching his clubs?

A. A banana, which *was* quite rotten when the caddie himself discovered it several months later.

Q. What longtime personal instructor to Jack Nicklaus died in 1989?

A. Jack Grout.

Q. Who was Greg Norman's fitness trainer in the late 1990s?

A. Pete Draovitch.

Q. Included among the clients of what agent are his brother-in-law (Tom Watson) and the Merry Mex (Lee Trevino)?

A. Chuck Rubin.

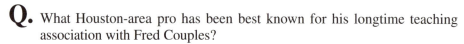

Q. What Houston-area pro has been best known for his longtime teaching association with Fred Couples?

A. Paul Marchand.

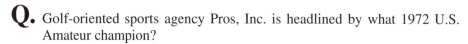

Q. Golf-oriented sports agency Pros, Inc. is headlined by what 1972 U.S. Amateur champion?

A. Marvin "Vinny" Giles.

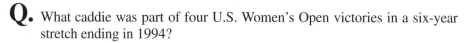

Q. What caddie was part of four U.S. Women's Open victories in a six-year stretch ending in 1994?

A. Carl Laib, who looped for Betsy King in 1989 and 1990, and for Patty Sheehan in 1992 and 1994.

Q. What shrewd agent who claimed to have brokered millions for both Greg Norman and Tiger Woods was dumped by both?

A. Hughes Norton III, of IMG.

Q. Walter Hagen's original manager was also what founder of *Golf World* magazine?

A. Bob Harlow.

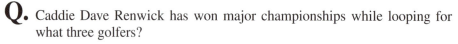

Q. Caddie Dave Renwick has won major championships while looping for what three golfers?

A. José Maria Olazábal (1994 Masters), Steve Elkington (1995 PGA Championship), and Vijay Singh (1998 PGA and 2000 Masters).

Q. One of golfer/teacher Mac O'Grady's first star pupils before they parted ways was what winner of five majors?

A. Seve Ballesteros.

———— ✕ ————

Q. What IMG rep immediately succeeded Hughes Norton III as Tiger Woods's manager in 1998?

A. Mark Steinberg.

———— ✕ ————

Q. What longtime caddie for Tom Watson left for a while to work for Greg Norman, only to return to Watson?

A. Bruce Edwards.

———— ✕ ————

Q. In the 1980s what teacher helped future Masters and British Open champion Mark O'Meara successfully revamp his swing?

A. Hank Haney.

———— ✕ ————

Q. What prominent sports-enhancement specialist (i.e., golf psychologist) laid the foundation for consulting with golfers by sending out a 187-page personal profile questionnaire to every tour player in 1989?

A. Dr. Deborah Graham.

———— ✕ ————

Q. Arnold Palmer and Tony Lema are among the British Open champs who employed what legendary caddie?

A. Tip Anderson.

———— ✕ ————

Q. Ben Crenshaw received what kind of final lesson from his mentor Harvey Penick in 1995, a week before Penick died and two weeks before Crenshaw broke out of a slump to win the Masters?

A. A putting lesson, in which Penick told his star pupil to make sure the putter head didn't pass his hands on the stroke.

Q. Who has been Tiger Woods's teacher since Woods turned pro in 1996?

A. Butch Harmon.

———∞———

Q. What longtime caddie of Lee Trevino's had a following of his own and even appeared in a TV commercial with Merry Mex, although he had to retire for health problems?

A. Herman Mitchell.

———∞———

Q. What longtime caddie for Jack Nicklaus was nicknamed the "Silver Greek"?

A. Angelo Argea.

———∞———

Q. Who was Francis Ouimet's pint-sized caddie when Ouimet won the 1913 U.S. Open?

A. Ten-year-old Eddie Lowery.

———∞———

Q. What sports agency with nifty vowel alliteration has handled a stable made for TV and entertainment, representing the likes of Gary McCord, David Feherty, Fuzzy Zoeller, and Chi Chi Rodriguez?

A. Eddie Elias Enterprises.

———∞———

Q. Earl Woods, Tiger's dad, caused a few nervous moments during a 1997 speaking engagement in Washington, D.C., when he gave what answer to a question about what book had been most inspirational to him?

A. Adolph Hitler's *Mein Kampf*, although Earl later insisted he was just joking. (Does that get Fuzzy Zoeller off the hook, too?)

———∞———

Q. Teacher David Leadbetter was born in what country?

A. England (but his family moved to Zimbabwe when he was six years old).

Q. What popular caddie, who carried John Daly and Nick Price to PGA Championships in back-to-back years, died in 1997?

A. Jeff "Squeeky" Medlen.

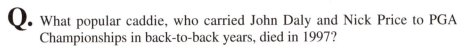

Q. What are the four C's upon which Dr. Bob Rotella has consistently based his competent consultation with clients?

A. Confidence, concentration, composure, and commitment.

Q. Caddie Dave Musgrove has won major championships with what three different golfers?

A. Seve Ballesteros, Sandy Lyle, and Lee Janzen.

Q. The father of what golfer, a former PGA Club Pro Championship winner, had a parking lot altercation with John Daly at the 1994 NEC World Series of Golf?

A. Jeff Roth.

Q. What star from another sport caddied for Mark Calcavecchia at the 1994 Western Open? (Hint: the Western Open is played near Chicago, but the "other" sport was not basketball.)

A. Ryne Sandberg, after his first retirement from the Chicago Cubs.

Q. What trick-shot artist often accompanied Walter Hagen on his worldwide exhibition tours?

A. Joe Kirkwood.

Q. What U.S. Amateur champ of the nineties had a prominent coach whose name sounds a lot like his?

A. 1998 winner Hank Kuehne played for Hank Haney, also a renowned teacher of pros, at Southern Methodist University.

Q. After working the 1986 Honda Classic, what caddie returned the next year as a contestant and won the darn thing?

A. Mark Calcavecchia, who had looped for Ken Green at the 1986 event.

Q. Teaching ace David Leadbetter had what two golfing superstars break off from him in 1998?

A. Nick Faldo and Se Ri Pak.

Q. What agent to John Daly has on occasion accompanied his client to meetings of Alcoholics Anonymous?

A. John Mascatello.

Q. What White House aide to Bill Clinton once commandeered the president's chopper to go play hookey at a nearby golf course?

A. David Watkins, an Arkansas millionaire who later had to cough up more than $13,000 to foot the bill.

Q. Caddie Joe Jones sued what golfer in 1996 for £15,000 over a pay dispute?

A. Seve Ballesteros. The case was thrown out of court.

Q. In recent decades who has been Arnold Palmer's personal assistant, handling many professional affairs such as media interviews?

A. Doc Giffin.

Q. What sports agency, represented by Ed Barner, beat IMG to the punch in the mid-seventies by signing emerging golf star Seve Ballesteros?

A. UMI (Uni-Managers International), whose other clients had included Johnny Miller and Billy Casper.

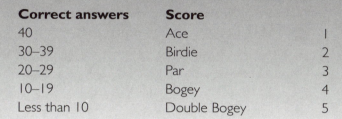

SCORECARD

40 Questions
Par: 3

Correct answers	Score	
40	Ace	1
30–39	Birdie	2
20–29	Par	3
10–19	Bogey	4
Less than 10	Double Bogey	5

Your score _____

14 PALMER, NICKLAUS, AND PLAYER

60 Questions
Par: 4

Q. In what branch of the service did Arnold Palmer enlist for a three-year stint?

A. Coast Guard.

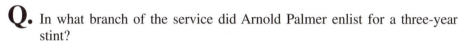

Q. Gary Player is known by what nickname shared by, among others, Johnny Cash?

A. "The Man in Black." (Count in Tommy Lee Jones and Will Smith, too.)

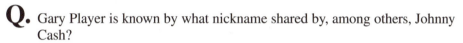

Q. Arnold Palmer earned the nickname "the King of the Desert" because of what achievement?

A. Arnie won more events "at the beach" than anyone else in history, with nine victories among the Hope, Phoenix, Tucson, Las Vegas, and the Sahara.

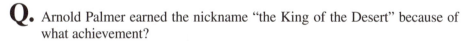

Q. Jack Nicklaus wrote an instructional book explaining how many ways to "lower your golf score"?

A. Fifty-five.

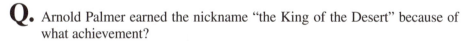

Q. Gary Player defeated what golfer in a play-off to win the 1965 U.S. Open?

A. Kel Nagle, of Australia.

Q. What has been Arnold Palmer's trademark clothing adjustment during the heat of battle, a move that always stirs his "army"?

A. Hitching up his pants.

Q. How many U.S. Amateurs did Palmer win?

A. One, in 1954.

Q. In 1990 Jack Nicklaus won what tournament, the first Senior PGA Tour event he entered?

A. The Tradition.

Q. Which of Gary Player's two sons has made a name for himself as a professional touring golfer?

A. Wayne Player.

Q. The only time Arnold Palmer won the U.S. Open, in 1960, who finished second?

A. Jack Nicklaus.

Q. Which of these three golfers, soon after visiting the Old Course at St. Andrews for the first time, remarked that the place should be "bulldozed into the sea"?

A. Gary Player, who had a change of heart when he became only the eleventh honorary member of the Royal and Ancient Golf Club of St. Andrews.

Q. Which of Nicklaus's twenty major victories (including his two U.S. Amateurs) was his fourteenth, moving him past Bobby Jones on the all-time majors' list?

A. The 1973 PGA Championship at Canterbury, outside Cleveland.

Q. What was the first name of Arnold Palmer's dad?

A. Although he went by Deacon (or Deke), it was actually Milfred.

Q. Gary Player was hit by a thrown telephone book, had ice flung at him, and had to putt while stray golf balls were rolled between his legs—among other things—courtesy of what kind of protesters at the 1969 PGA Championship?

A. Anti-apartheid. Player, a native of South Africa, managed to finish second, one shot behind winner Raymond Floyd.

Q. Where did Arnold Palmer attend college?

A. Wake Forest.

Q. Palmer was a golf commentator for what network in the late 1970s?

A. NBC.

Q. What two players did Jack Nicklaus beat in a play-off to win the 1966 Masters?

A. Gay Brewer and Tommy Jacobs.

Q. Which one of these big three is the only one to have won British Opens in three different decades?

A. Gary Player, who won British Opens in 1959, 1968, and 1974.

Q. How many individual Atlantic Coast Conference golf titles did Arnold Palmer win while at Wake Forest?

A. Three.

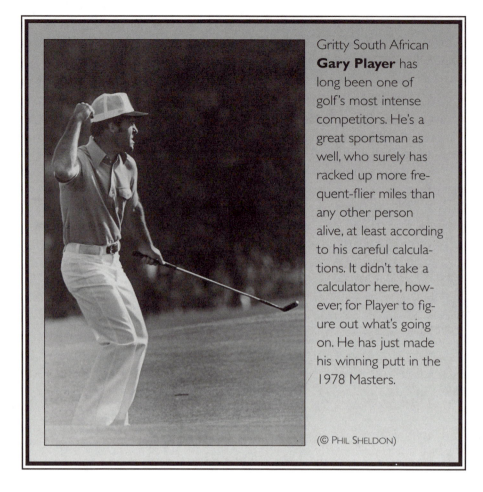

Gritty South African **Gary Player** has long been one of golf's most intense competitors. He's a great sportsman as well, who surely has racked up more frequent-flier miles than any other person alive, at least according to his careful calculations. It didn't take a calculator here, however, for Player to figure out what's going on. He has just made his winning putt in the 1978 Masters.

(© PHIL SHELDON)

Q. Palmer's first victory on the PGA Tour came in what event?

A. The 1955 Canadian Open.

Q. What are the names of Jack Nicklaus's four sons?

A. Jack II ("Jackie"), Steven, Gary, and Michael.

Q. The PGA Tour's Arnold Palmer Award is given annually to whom?

A. The tour's leading money winner.

Q. At the 1983 Skins Game, what fellow competitor caused a ruckus by claiming that Gary Player had cheated by repositioning a "growing live weed leaf" behind his ball?

A. Tom Watson. Player admitted he moved the leaf, but only to confirm that it was attached to the ground and was not a loose impediment.

Q. What is the name of Jack Nicklaus's daughter?

A. Nancy Jean.

Q. Arnold Palmer has been the recipient of an award named after what past U.S. Open champion whose legacy includes a scholarship program for caddies?

A. Francis Ouimet.

Q. When was the last time Palmer and Nicklaus went head-to-head in a play-off at a tour event?

A. The 1970 Byron Nelson Classic. Nicklaus won on the first hole of sudden death.

Q. Palmer birdied the last two holes of the 1960 Masters to vault past what golfer and win?

A. Ken Venturi.

Q. What is the title of Gary Player's book about staying in shape, released in paperback in 1995?

A. *Fit for Golf.*

Q. Tony Lema defeated Arnold Palmer in a play-off at the 1964 Cleveland Open using a putter that had been loaned to him by what golfer?

A. Arnold Palmer.

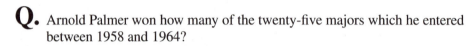

Q. As a young adult growing up in Columbus, Ohio, Nicklaus worked part-time alongside his father, Charlie, in what business?

A. A pharmacy.

Q. Arnold Palmer won how many of the twenty-five majors which he entered between 1958 and 1964?

A. Seven.

Q. What is the maiden name of Jack Nicklaus's wife?

A. Barbara Bash.

Q. What are the names of Arnold Palmer's two daughters?

A. Peggy and Amy.

Q. Gary Player won each of the four regular majors at least twice except for which one?

A. The U.S. Open. His only victory there came in 1965.

Q. How old was Arnold Palmer when he shot his age for the first time in competition?

A. Sixty-six, in the final round of the 1995 GTE Northwest Classic.

One aspect of **Arnold Palmer**'s enduring appeal has been his willingness to wear his emotions on his sleeve, whether it be disappointment or joy.

(COURTESY OF LIBRARY OF CONGRESS)

Q. Which of Jack Nicklaus's four sons was caddying for Dad when the "Olden Bear" won the 1986 Masters at age forty-six?

A. Jack Jr. ("Jackie").

Q. Arnold Palmer's last regular PGA Tour victory came when and where?

A. At the 1973 Bob Hope Desert Classic.

Q. At age ten Jack Nicklaus shot what nine-hole score in his first try at golf?

A. 51.

Q. Gary Player came from seven shots back of whom to win the 1978 Masters?

A. Hubert Green.

Q. Jack Nicklaus won both the 1970 National Four-Ball and the 1971 National Team with what playing partner?

A. Arnold Palmer.

Q. Nicklaus's 275 total in winning the 1967 U.S. Open bettered whose previous Open-scoring record by one stroke?

A. Ben Hogan's.

Q. Gary Player's dad, Harry, worked in what occupational field?

A. Mining.

Q. When Nicklaus announced at age twenty-one he was turning pro, he received a cable from what legendary amateur golfer pleading for him to reconsider?

A. Bobby Jones.

Q. In what year was Arnold Palmer born?

A. 1929.

Q. How many career "regular" PGA Tour victories does Jack Nicklaus have?

A. Seventy.

Q. Gary Player's first PGA Tour victory came in what event appropriate to his love of and work with horses?

A. The 1958 Kentucky Derby Open.

Jack Nicklaus celebrates yet another triumph, this one at the 1963 Masters.

(COURTESY OF LIBRARY OF CONGRESS)

Q. Arnold Palmer is the principal owner of what Florida facility that is the host site of a PGA Tour event?

A. Bay Hill Club and Lodge.

Q. Why are Arnold Palmer and Jack Nicklaus both still exempt for the regular PGA Tour?

A. By winning the U.S. Open when it still carried a lifetime PGA Tour exemption: Palmer in 1960, Nicklaus in 1962.

Q. Gary Player won what 1998 Senior Tour event at age sixty-two?

A. The Northville Long Island Classic.

Q. Who held the lead going into the final round of the 1960 U.S. Open, considered perhaps the greatest major ever in that its leader board was a place of convergence for the cross-generational likes of Arnold Palmer, Jack Nicklaus, and Ben Hogan?

A. Mike Souchak. Palmer ended up winning.

Q. In what tournament did Gary Player win for the first time outside his native South Africa?

A. The 1955 Egyptian Match Play.

Q. Arnold Palmer's last major victory on the regular PGA Tour came in what event?

A. The 1964 Masters.

Q. In which two years did Jack Nicklaus win his own tournament, the Memorial?

A. 1977 and 1984.

Q. With which of his four sons did Nicklaus compete in the 1997 U.S. Open?

A. Gary.

Q. In what year did Gary Player win two majors?

A. 1974; the Masters and British Open.

Q. In 1966 when Jack Nicklaus became the first Masters winner to successfully defend his title at Augusta, how did tournament cochairmen Bobby Jones and Clifford Roberts handle the tradition whereby the previous year's winner helps the new winner put on his green jacket?

A. Nicklaus put the coat on all by himself.

Eight Times During the 1960s, Major Tournaments Featured a One-Two Finish from among Palmer, Nicklaus, and Player

1. 1960 U.S. Open: Palmer first, Nicklaus second
2. 1961 Masters: Player first, Palmer tied for second
3. 1962 Masters: Palmer first, Player tied for second
4. 1962 U.S. Open: Nicklaus first, Palmer second
5. 1964 Masters: Palmer first, Nicklaus tied for second
6. 1965 Masters: Nicklaus first, Palmer and Player tied for second
7. 1967 U.S. Open: Nicklaus first, Palmer second
8. 1968 British Open: Player first, Nicklaus tied for second

Q. When Arnold Palmer won the first Senior PGA Tour event in which he participated, whom did he beat in a play-off?

A. Paul Harney, in the 1980 Senior Players' Championship.

Q. Gary Player won his first Senior PGA Tour start in what event?

A. The 1985 Quadel Classic.

Q. Who were the only two men other than Palmer, Nicklaus, or Player to win a PGA Tour money title during the sixties?

A. Billy Casper (1966 and 1968) and Frank Beard (1969).

Q. The maiden names of the wives of Palmer, Nicklaus, and Player have what in common?

A. All are alliterative: Winnie Walzer, Barbara Bash, and Vivienne Verwey, respectively.

14

SCORECARD

60 Questions
Par: 4

Correct answers	Score	
58–60	Eagle	2
45–57	Birdie	3
30–44	Par	4
20–29	Bogey	5
10–19	Double Bogey	6
Less than 10	Triple Bogey	7

Your score _____

15 GOLF MEDIA AND POP CULTURE

80 Questions
Par: 5

Q. Who was *The Bogey Man*?

A. Writer George Plimpton, whose book detailing his real-life stab at competitive golf was published in 1968.

⟨∞⟩

Q. Who succeeded Frank Chirkinian as CBS-TV's golf producer?

A. Lance Barrow.

⟨∞⟩

Q. Who was the first golfer named Man of the Year by *Sports Illustrated*?

A. Arnold Palmer, in 1960.

⟨∞⟩

Q. Ben Hogan's best-selling instructional *Five Lessons: The Modern Fundamentals of Golf* featured the artwork of what illustrator?

A. Anthony Ravielli.

⟨∞⟩

Q. What longtime and legendary TV golf analyst served in the British Parliament for several years in the 1940s?

A. Henry Longhurst.

Q. What is the title of Jack Nicklaus's 1997 autobiography?

A. *My Story.*

———⧈———

Q. What fellow Texan collaborated with Harvey Penick on his best-selling books?

A. Bud Shrake.

———⧈———

Q. Sports psychologist Dr. Bob Rotella's first book on golf had what title?

A. *Golf Is Not a Game of Perfect* (with Bob Cullen).

———⧈———

Q. The original core members of the (so-called) musical group Jake Trout and the Flounders were what three golfers?

A. Peter Jacobsen (Jake), Payne Stewart, and Mark Lye.

———⧈———

Q. Bill Murray's greenkeeper "Carl," an "unknown out of nowhere," used what club to hole out a 190-yard shot to win his fantasy Masters in *Caddyshack?*

A. Eight-iron.

———⧈———

Q. What grandson of a famous evolutionist authored such golf books as *A Friendly Round* and *Golf Between Two Wars?*

A. Bernard Darwin, whose granddad Charles Darwin wrote the controversial *On the Origin of Species.*

———⧈———

Q. What well-known golfer and TV golf analyst made a cameo appearance in the movie *Tin Cup* alongside Kevin Costner in a driving-range scene?

A. Johnny Miller.

Henry Longhurst touched about every base there is in the world of golf journalism. Here he's at "work" for the *London Sunday Times*. American golf fans remember him best for his color commentary on CBS-TV.

(© PHIL SHELDON)

Q. In the late nineties, what award-winning golf writer for the *New York Times*, *Golf World*, and *The National* joined Callaway as a vice president?

A. Larry Dorman.

Q. Against what screen villain did Sean Connery's James Bond play the match of his life?

A. Goldfinger.

Q. What is the name of Nick Faldo's 1995 instructional book?

A. *Faldo! In Search of Perfection.*

———∞———

Q. What three-time British Open champion faithfully wrote a newspaper column for more than thirty years?

A. Henry Cotton.

———∞———

Q. What fiery and outspoken NFL coach whose career has detoured through television broadcasting spent some time helping NBC cover golf?

A. Mike Ditka, a single-digit handicapper at golf.

———∞———

Q. Five years after winning an Oscar, what actress portrayed Ben Hogan's wife Valerie in the 1951 flick *Follow the Sun*?

A. Anne Baxter (Best Supporting Actress Oscar winner in 1946 for *The Razor's Edge*).

———∞———

Q. Where did CBS-TV golf anchor Jim Nantz play his collegiate golf?

A. University of Houston. Fred Couples and Blaine McCallister were two of his teammates.

———∞———

Q. What two-time U.S. Amateur Women's champion wrote the 1904 book *Golf for Women*?

A. Genevieve Hecker.

———∞———

Q. What television actor, who had a prominent role on a highly rated sixties sitcom, cowrote a golf comedy screenplay called *The Sweet Spot*?

A. Max Baer Jr., aka Jethro Bodine from *The Beverly Hillbillies*.

Q. Why did golfer Ben Crenshaw turn down a supporting role in the film version of *Dead Solid Perfect*, based on the book written by fellow Texan Dan Jenkins?

A. Because of the "blue" language in the film, Crenshaw said.

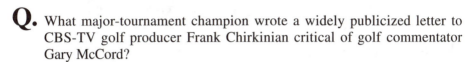

Q. What major-tournament champion wrote a widely publicized letter to CBS-TV golf producer Frank Chirkinian critical of golf commentator Gary McCord?

A. Tom Watson.

Q. The 1936 film short *Divot Diggers* about incompetent caddies starred what well-known group of actors?

A. "Our Gang," the trio of Spanky, Alfalfa, and Buckwheat.

Q. What veteran actor is credited as the coauthor of *The Stupid Little Golf Book*?

A. Leslie Nielsen, joined by the hilarious Henry Beard.

Q. Although commonly referred to as *The Little Green Book*, what's the actual title of Harvey Penick's successful sequel to the enormously popular *Harvey Penick's Little Red Book*?

A. *...And If You Play Golf, You're My Friend.*

Q. What actor's Judge Boggs character used a golf club as a gavel in the 1992 TV melodrama *Grass Roots*?

A. Old "Ironside" himself, Raymond Burr.

Q. Who immediately preceded Dick Enberg as NBC-TV's golf anchor?

A. Jim Lampley.

Q. CBS-TV's first Masters-coverage addition after commentator Gary McCord was bounced by the Augusta brass was what other tour veteran?

A. Jim Nelford.

Q. In 1994 what longtime CBS-TV golf anchor left his spot atop the tower at eighteen and bolted to Fox to follow NFL telecasts there?

A. Pat Summerall.

Q. Katharine Hepburn and Cary Grant hit the links in what 1938 romantic comedy?

A. *Bringing Up Baby.*

Q. What wife of Cary Grant's had a starring role in a movie comedy about golf?

A. Dyan Cannon, in *Caddyshack II.*

Q. Tiger Woods was quoted in what magazine making jokes that could be construed as offensive to lesbians and blacks?

A. *Gentleman's Quarterly.*

Q. In an act of self-sabotage, CBS's Ben Wright made politically incorrect comments about the LPGA and women golfers to what newspaper journalist?

A. Valerie Helmbreck, of the *Wilmington (Delaware) News Journal.*

Q. What's the title of the 1993 unauthorized Arnold Palmer biography written by Larry Guest?

A. *Arnie: Inside the Legend.*

A Good Phrase Spoiled

When Samuel Clemens, aka Mark Twain, added the immortal phrase "Golf is a good walk spoiled" to our cultural history, little could he have known just how catchy those words would be. Be careful next time you go to a bookstore and place an order for a book with a title that includes "A Good Walk Spoiled." There are at least three of them released in a span of six years in the 1990s. First there was *Golf Is a Good Walk Spoiled* by George Eberl and C. Grant Spaeth, published in 1992. Then came John Feinstein's best-selling chronicling of life on the PGA Tour, published in 1996 under the full title *A Good Walk Spoiled: Days and Nights on the PGA Tour*. Finally, in 1998, the world of book publishing welcomed Helen Exley's *Golf . . . a Good Walk Spoiled*. If you somehow end up receiving the wrong book from the bookstore, take solace in the fact you, presumably, drove your car to get there. Otherwise, your pedestrian trip would have been, shall we say—oh, never mind.

Q. When he missed the ball and awkwardly struck the ground while practicing golf, what prominent college basketball TV analyst fractured a wrist?

A. Dick Vitale.

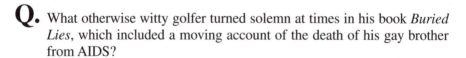

Q. What otherwise witty golfer turned solemn at times in his book *Buried Lies*, which included a moving account of the death of his gay brother from AIDS?

A. Peter Jacobsen.

Q. During the Army ROTC drill scene in *Animal House,* we see Boone and Otter each hit two golf shots that end up where?

A. Boone's two wild shots land in a soup kettle and in Dean Wormer's office; Otter's dead-solid-perfect shots hit the back end of Neidermeyer's horse and then Neidermeyer's helmeted head.

Q. What nineties TV sitcom character won a fictitious Titleist hole-in-one award for knocking a ball into a whale's blowhole?

A. Kramer, of *Seinfeld*.

———

Q. Phil Mickelson once made a cameo appearance on what hour-long TV show to give an out-of-this-world guy a golf lesson?

A. *Lois and Clark*, costarring Dean Cain as golf student Clark Kent/Superman.

———

Q. What *Golf Digest* staffer wrote the book *My Kingdom for a Groove*?

A. Marcia Chambers.

———

Q. What country music star, himself a near-scratch golfer, dedicated his 1993 album *I Still Believe in You* to Heather Farr, who eventually succumbed to cancer?

A. Vince Gill.

———

Q. What match-play partner of Judge Smales's in *Caddyshack* had won multiple club championships at Bushwood?

A. Dr. Beeper.

———

Q. With what publisher did Tiger Woods sign a two-book deal for a reported $2.2 million in 1996?

A. Warner Books.

———

Q. What was the name of the Golf Channel's thirty-minute pretournament show that was axed in 1995 only five months after the network's launch?

A. *Golf Today*.

Q. The book *Michael and Me: Our Gambling Addiction . . . My Cry for Help!*, written by Richard Esquinas, accused what prominent athlete of a golf-gambling addiction to the tune of $1.25 million allegedly owed Esquinas?

A. Michael Jordan.

Q. Who wrote *Golf in the Kingdom*?

A. Michael Murphy.

Q. What avid Hollywood golfer bought the movie rights to *Golf in the Kingdom*, supposedly planning to star himself in the flick version?

A. Clint Eastwood.

Q. What sports psychologist wrote the book *Mind over Golf*?

A. Dr. Richard Coop.

Q. What actor played the lead role of guzzling golfer Kenny Lee Puckett in the film version of *Dead Solid Perfect*?

A. Randy Quaid.

Q. What network TV golf analyst preceded David Fay as the USGA's executive director?

A. Frank Hannigan.

Q. Who starred in the 1930 flick *The Golf Specialist*, about a golf pro trying to teach a woman how to play golf?

A. W. C. Fields.

Q. In his first AT&T Pebble Beach National Pro-Am, who was Tiger Woods's celebrity amateur partner?

A. Kevin Costner.

―――∞∞∞―――

Q. Which of the seven marooned folks on *Gilligan's Island* was the most avid golfer?

A. Thurston Howell III.

―――∞∞∞―――

Q. What 1996 book authored by Carl Vigeland apparently tried to dupe readers into thinking it was some sort of Greg Norman biography by its title and cover photo showing Norman lining up a putt?

A. *Stalking the Shark.*

―――∞∞∞―――

Q. What was the familial link between entertainer Jackie Gleason and the 1996 U.S. Senior Open?

A. One of the contestants was Gleason's real-life first cousin Jimmy Gleason.

―――∞∞∞―――

Q. What longtime golf writer and editor (who died the same week as Ben Hogan) was the first recipient of the PGA Lifetime Achievement Award in Journalism?

A. Dick Taylor.

―――∞∞∞―――

Q. What TV journalist, himself a golf aficionado, forked out $8,000 at a 1997 charity auction for a day with Tiger Woods at a junior clinic?

A. Bryant Gumbel.

―――∞∞∞―――

Q. Who authored the poignant bestseller *Final Rounds*?

A. James Dodson.

Mr. Sandbagger

If a Hollywood producer ever gets an itch to do a movie about sand-bagging at golf, he might consider casting **Andy Garcia** in the lead role. Garcia, who's had starring roles in flicks such as *The Untouchables*, pulled off what could be construed as the "unimpossible" at the 1996 AT&T Pebble Beach National Pro-Am. Claiming an amateur's handicap of 14 (further adjusted higher for course difficulty), Garcia played like a pro that week, shooting, by some witness accounts, in the 70s at both Pebble Beach and Poppy Hills. He teamed with real pro Paul Stankowski to win the pro-am portion of the tournament at 43 under par. Touchable? Not that week, at least.

Q. The 1948 flick *My Bunny Lies Over the Sea* introduced what cartoon character to golf?

A. Bugs Bunny.

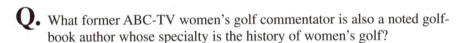

Q. What former ABC-TV women's golf commentator is also a noted golf-book author whose specialty is the history of women's golf?

A. Rhonda Glenn.

Q. Arnold Haultain's book *The Mystery of Golf*, published in 1908, was one of the first books to explore what field of science relative to golf?

A. Psychology.

Q. What late CBS golf commentator and former sportswriter known for his informative yet humorous weekly pieces was once described as "the Andy Rooney of golf"?

A. Bob Drum.

Q. After Rodney Dangerfield turned down a role in the sequel *Caddyshack II*, he was replaced by what fellow comedian portraying a wisecracking real-estate developer with a distaste for country club snobs?

A. Jackie Mason.

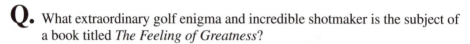

Q. What longtime TV golf commentator was born in Germany, has a British accent, and played in eight Ryder Cup Matches?

A. Peter Alliss.

Q. What extraordinary golf enigma and incredible shotmaker is the subject of a book titled *The Feeling of Greatness*?

A. Moe Norman.

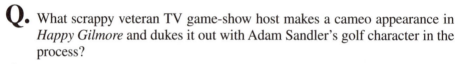

Q. What scrappy veteran TV game-show host makes a cameo appearance in *Happy Gilmore* and dukes it out with Adam Sandler's golf character in the process?

A. Bob Barker.

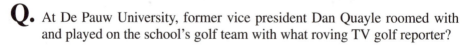

Q. What is the title of author Michael Murphy's sequel to his cult classic book *Golf in the Kingdom*?

A. *The Kingdom of Shivas Irons.*

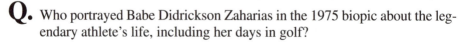

Q. At De Pauw University, former vice president Dan Quayle roomed with and played on the school's golf team with what roving TV golf reporter?

A. Mark Rolfing.

———— ⊗⊗⊗ ————

Q. Who portrayed Babe Didrickson Zaharias in the 1975 biopic about the legendary athlete's life, including her days in golf?

A. Susan Clark.

Q. Who was the original *Sports Illustrated* golf writer who went on to write for the *New Yorker* for forty years?

A. Herbert Warren Wind.

———∞∞∞———

Q. Homer Simpson got a golf lesson from what former U.S. Open champion guest-voicing on an episode of *The Simpsons*?

A. Tom Kite.

———∞∞∞———

Q. Moe, Larry, and Curly starred in what film featuring golf?

A. *Three Little Bears*.

———∞∞∞———

Q. What PGA Tour pro, and presumed golf expert, was listed as a consultant for the movie *Happy Gilmore*, which included scenes of a golf fan driving a car onto a golf course during a tournament, Gilmore getting a mere bogey for a hole on which he had several whiffs and found the water, and a bogus ruling that required a shot off the shoe of a spectator without a drop?

A. Mark "I Never Tell A" Lye.

———∞∞∞———

Q. In what Bob Hope movie did Arnold Palmer make a cameo appearance as a golfer who interrupts breakfast with a stray golf shot?

A. *Call Me Bwana*.

———∞∞∞———

Q. What actor played the title role in the 1998 Showtime flick *The Tiger Woods Story*?

A. Khalil Kain.

———∞∞∞———

Q. Why did golfer Chi Chi Rodriguez file a lawsuit against Universal Pictures over its 1995 release of *To Wong Foo Thanks for Everything Julie Newmar*?

A. A drag-queen character in the movie was named Chi Chi Rodriguez, without the Cheech's permission.

Q. What ghoulish rock star whose heydey was the pre-disco seventies has been a Callaway pitchman in the nineties?

A. Alice Cooper, who carries a single-digit handicap.

Q. Who succeeded Brent Musberger as ABC-TV's golf anchor?

A. Mike Tirico.

Q. A U.S. president is kidnapped during a round of golf and replaced by an actor in what 1967 movie starring James Coburn?

A. *In Like Flint.*

15

SCORECARD
80 Questions
Par: 5

Correct answers	Score	
78–80	Double eagle	2
70–77	Eagle	3
55–69	Birdie	4
40–54	Par	5
30–39	Bogey	6
15–29	Double Bogey	7
Less than 15	Triple Bogey	8

Your score _____

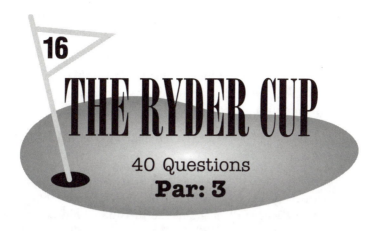

THE RYDER CUP

40 Questions
Par: 3

Q. What unassuming winner of two PGA Championships and one U.S. Open amassed a perfect 9-0 record in his first two Ryder Cups, in 1979 and 1981?

A. Larry Nelson.

Q. Who was the captain of the last British team to win the Ryder Cup before the competition was expanded to include all of Europe?

A. Dai Rees, in 1957.

Q. What was at the heart of the 1989 Ryder Cup controversy at the Belfry involving Paul Azinger and his European singles opponent Seve Ballesteros, after Azinger hit his tee shot at eighteen into the water?

A. Azinger's subsequent drop, which Ballesteros later claimed was wrong. Azinger halved the hole and won his crucial match against Seve.

Q. When was the last time brothers were represented on the same Ryder Cup team?

A. 1963, when Bernard and Geoffrey Hunt were teammates on the Great Britain-Ireland squad.

Q. Who was the first Dane to play in the Ryder Cup?

A. Thomas Bjorn, in 1997.

Q. What became of the two-iron that Irishman Christy O'Connor Jr. used to hit the magnificent approach shot at Belfry's eighteenth to finish off Fred Couples in their climactic 1989 singles match?

A. O'Connor sold it for £50,000 and then donated the money to a hospice.

Q. A 1997 controversy involved the removal of what Spanish golfer from the European team because of an injury he insisted would not prevent him from playing in the Matches?

A. Miguel Angel Martin.

Q. In 1985 when the Europeans bushwhacked the Americans, 16½–11½, to bring Europe its first Ryder Cup team triumph in twenty-eight years, who was in the wrong place at the wrong time as U.S. captain?

A. Lee Trevino.

Q. The Ryder Cup is named after whom?

A. Samuel A. Ryder, a wealthy British seed merchant.

Q. ABC-TV golf commentator Peter Alliss had a hand in designing what oft-used Ryder Cup venue?

A. The Belfry, in England.

Q. In 1985 what European came back from three down with eight holes to play to win what proved to be the clinching point for his team?

A. Sam Torrance, against reigning U.S. Open champ Andy North.

Q. In what year did the Americans win on British soil for the first time?

A. 1937.

A Chip off the Old Beck

Chip Beck often gets a bad rap for what he did, or actually didn't do, in laying up at the fifteenth hole while in final-round contention at the 1993 Masters. But that's probably okay with an eternally upbeat guy like Beck, who has an uncanny ability to see a glass half full of water even when it's empty. Such was the case at the 1993 Ryder Cup Matches, where Beck patiently rode the pine for the first three rounds before coming off that Saturday afternoon to team up with John Cook in defeating Europe's formidable Nick Faldo-Colin Montgomerie pairing, thus winning a crucial four-ball match. Then on Sunday, Beck was three holes down with five to go in his singles match against Barry Lane when he mounted a comeback that gave him a one-up victory over Lane and inspired the Americans to victory. Beck's mantra all that week was "You gotta love it," and a lot of people on the west side of the Atlantic did. Say what you will about Mister 59 Jr., but Beck's a good guy to have in your foxhole when the artillery is in the air.

Q. What over-forty American making his Ryder Cup debut in 1997 had a winning individual record, even though the Yanks lost—again?

A. Scott Hoch.

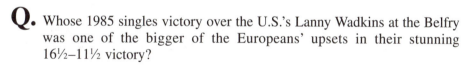

Q. Whose 1985 singles victory over the U.S.'s Lanny Wadkins at the Belfry was one of the bigger of the Europeans' upsets in their stunning 16½–11½ victory?

A. Manuel Piñero.

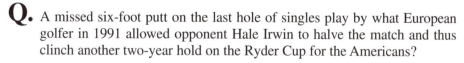

Q. A missed six-foot putt on the last hole of singles play by what European golfer in 1991 allowed opponent Hale Irwin to halve the match and thus clinch another two-year hold on the Ryder Cup for the Americans?

A. Bernhard Langer.

Q. American team captain Ben Hogan was barbecued by the British press in 1949 for bringing over what cargo for his team to eat in the tightly rationed British Isles?

A. Six hundred pounds of meat.

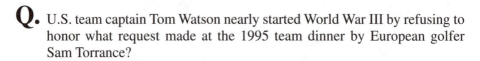

Q. U.S. team captain Tom Watson nearly started World War III by refusing to honor what request made at the 1995 team dinner by European golfer Sam Torrance?

A. To autograph Torrance's dinner menu.

Q. Future CBS-TV golf commentator David Feherty scored a two-and-one victory over what American stalwart in the 1991 Ryder Cup?

A. Payne Stewart.

Q. In terms of percentage of total points won, in what Ryder Cup year did the United States score its most lopsided victory?

A. 1947, with an 11–1 score.

Q. Who stiffed a wedge shot to within eighteen inches on the last hole in 1983 to win the hole, halve his match, and clinch a nail-biting victory for the United States?

A. Lanny Wadkins.

Q. Who was the captain of the 1981 American team, the last U.S. squad to win the Ryder Cup by a comfortable margin (18½–9½)?

A. Dave Marr, whose team that year included Jack Nicklaus, Lee Trevino, and Tom Watson.

Q. In 1991 whose four-up lead on Europe's Colin Montgomerie with four holes to play evaporated completely when he played the last four holes in eight over par?

A. Mark Calcavecchia.

Q. Although he had the consolation of winning that year's British Open, whose three-putt on the final hole in the 1933 Ryder Cup cost the Americans the Cup?

A. Denny Shute.

Q. American patriot Corey Pavin paid his respects to his fellow countrymen who had served during the Gulf War by wearing what adornment during the 1991 Ryder Cup Match at Kiawah Island, South Carolina?

A. A Desert Storm service hat.

Q. What European star was conspicuous by his absence from the 1981 Ryder Cup team, after he temporarily resigned his membership in the European Tour over a dispute regarding appearance money?

A. Seve Ballesteros.

Q. What American in the late 1990s expressed his apparent apathy for the Ryder Cup by reportedly saying, "My goal is to be the first person to become eligible for the Ryder Cup and politely decline"?

A. Bill Glasson.

Q. Loren Roberts fired his caddie Dan Stojak around the time of the 1995 Ryder Cup for what reason?

A. Stojak had placed a bet on the Europeans to win.

This is not evidence of the thrill of victory. It's Germany's **Bernhard Langer** expressing the agony of defeat for all of Europe, having just missed a six-foot putt on the final green during the final singles match of the 1991 Ryder Cup Matches at Kiawah Island. Langer's missed putt allowed opponent Hale Irwin to get the half-point needed to push the Yanks over the top to victory. (© PHIL SHELDON)

Q. Where were the first official Ryder Cup Matches contested?

A. Worcester Country Club, Worcester, Massachusetts, in 1927.

Q. In the percentage of total points won, the Europeans scored their most lop-sided victory in what Ryder Cup year?

A. 1957, when the Brits/Irish won, 7½ to 4½.

Q. After making a five-foot putt himself, Jack Nicklaus conceded a three-foot putt to what European counterpart in the 1969 Ryder Cup, securing the Europeans a tie and making a few Americans mutter under their collective breath?

A. Tony Jacklin.

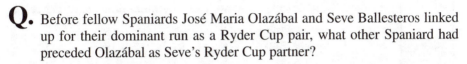

Q. Before fellow Spaniards José Maria Olazábal and Seve Ballesteros linked up for their dominant run as a Ryder Cup pair, what other Spaniard had preceded Olazábal as Seve's Ryder Cup partner?

A. Manuel Piñero, who teamed with Ballesteros to win three of their four two-man matches at the 1985 event.

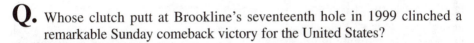

Q. Whose clutch putt at Brookline's seventeenth hole in 1999 clinched a remarkable Sunday comeback victory for the United States?

A. Justin Leonard.

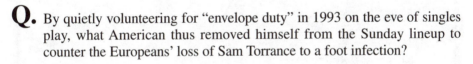

Q. By quietly volunteering for "envelope duty" in 1993 on the eve of singles play, what American thus removed himself from the Sunday lineup to counter the Europeans' loss of Sam Torrance to a foot infection?

A. Lanny Wadkins.

Q. Who succeeded 1997 European team captain Seve Ballesteros in that same position?

A. Mark James.

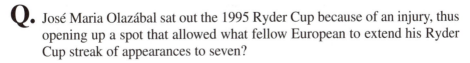

Q. José Maria Olazábal sat out the 1995 Ryder Cup because of an injury, thus opening up a spot that allowed what fellow European to extend his Ryder Cup streak of appearances to seven?

A. Ian Woosnam.

Quick Thinker

As far as American golf historians are concerned, the Ryder Cup probably deserves to be nicknamed the "Hagen Cup," for it was the legendary **Walter Hagen** of the United States who had as much to do with the early success of the Ryder Cup as anybody. Hagen, the best American professional golfer of that era, helped organize the unofficial 1926 intercontinental competition that begat the Ryder Cup starting in 1927. Hagen served as captain of the first six American squads in the biennial competition. He handpicked the team members and selected the uniforms, paying for them out of his own pocket. A connoisseur of all things fine and elegant (and expensive), Hagen was in no way a greedy man, and he cherished this opportunity to bestow such gifts of clothing and great golf competition on his fellow Yanks. Home-course advantage prevailed in each of the first five matches, before the United States broke through in 1937 to win, 8–4, at Southport, England. A quick thinker on the course and off, Hagen got the chance to play a nice recovery after he misspoke at the awards ceremony, when he said, "I am proud and happy to be captain of the first American team to win on home soil." When a heckler reminded Hagen that the Americans were the guests, not the hosts, Hagen deftly countered, "You will forgive me, I am sure, for feeling so at home here." Touché, for Hagen had indeed made himself right at home in Great Britain, winning four British Open Championships between 1922 and 1929.

Q. Who was the only reigning and otherwise eligible American major tournament winner denied a spot on the Ryder Cup team—twice?

A. John Daly, who failed to get a captain's nod in either 1991 (when he won the PGA Championship) or 1995 (British Open). He wasn't a top-ten point-getter either time around.

———◯◯◯———

Q. In what year was a European country other than England host of the Ryder Cup Matches?

A. 1973, at Muirfield, in Scotland.

Q. What U.S. Ryder Cup captain of the 1990s had a tidy 5-0-2 record in singles play in seven Cup appearances as a player?

A. Tom Kite.

Q. Who in effect earned himself a nice, self-served bonus of £2,500 by scoring the clinching point in the Europeans' stunning 1995 upset of the Americans?

A. Philip Walton, who had bet £1,000 on his team at five-to-two odds before flying to America for the event.

Q. Who was the last American to serve consecutive terms as U.S. Ryder Cup captain?

A. Walter Hagen, who served six straight times from 1927 through 1937.

16

SCORECARD

40 Questions
Par: 3

Correct answers	Score	
40	Ace	1
30–39	Birdie	2
20–29	Par	3
10–19	Bogey	4
Less than 10	Double Bogey	5

Your score _____

FALDO, NORMAN, AND BALLESTEROS

17

50 Questions
Par: 4

Q. What is Seve Ballesteros's real first name?

A. Severiano.

———— ∞ ————

Q. Nick Faldo's first PGA Tour victory on American soil came where?

A. At the Sea Pines Heritage Classic, in 1984.

———— ∞ ————

Q. What is the name of Greg Norman's company?

A. Great White Shark Enterprises.

———— ∞ ————

Q. In 1997 what American moved to number one in the World Rankings, ending Norman's ninety-six-week stay at the top?

A. Tom Lehman.

———— ∞ ————

Q. Presumably in recognition of the setting of three of his major victories, Nick Faldo gave what name to his third child?

A. Georgia, where he won three Masters Tournaments.

Q. Ever since Greg Norman cut his ties with IMG in 1993, who has been his business manager?

A. Frank Williams.

———— ❦ ————

Q. What is Nick Faldo's full name?

A. Nicholas Alexander Faldo.

———— ❦ ————

Q. What is the name of the Spanish fishing village in which Seve Ballesteros grew up?

A. Pedreña.

———— ❦ ————

Q. In an emotional ceremony, Greg Norman dedicated his victory in the 1988 Heritage Classic to what cancer-stricken boy?

A. Jamie Hutton.

———— ❦ ————

Q. With what final-round score did Seve Ballesteros win his third British Open, in 1988?

A. 65, at Royal Lytham and St. Anne's.

———— ❦ ————

Q. Greg Norman said he was pretty much a self-taught golfer who learned from the instructional scrolls of what great linkster?

A. Jack Nicklaus.

———— ❦ ————

Q. About how much moolah did Norman pocket when Cobra (to include his shares) was sold to American Brands?

A. $40 million.

Q. Of Nick Faldo's six PGA Tour victories through 1998, which was the only one outside the southeastern United States?

A. The 1997 Nissan Open, in California.

Q. What equipment company signed Faldo to a "lifetime" contract in 1998?

A. Adams Golf.

Q. What drastic action did Seve Ballesteros's dad, Baldomero, take long ago to avoid fighting in the Spanish Civil War?

A. He shot himself in the hand.

Q. How old was Seve when he won the Masters for the first time, in 1980?

A. Twenty-three.

Q. How tall is Greg Norman?

A. Six feet, even.

Q. Where did Norman grow up?

A. Queensland, Australia.

Q. Seve Ballesteros broke a long victory drought by winning what European PGA Tour event in May 1994?

A. Benson and Hedges International.

Q. Nick Faldo's play-off opponents when he won consecutive Masters Tournaments were what two Americans?

A. Scott Hoch in 1989 and Raymond Floyd in 1990.

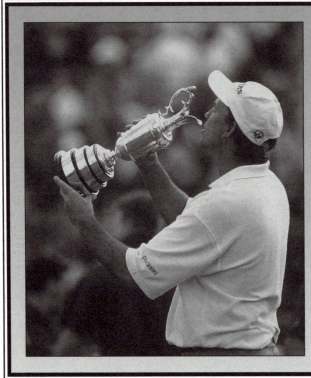

Years of struggling to make it on the PGA Tour finally came to fruition in the 1990s for **Tom Lehman**, seen here indulging a wee bit after winning the 1996 British Open, his first major triumph. A few months later Lehman knocked Greg Norman off the number one perch in the World Rankings.

(JAN TRAYLEN PHOTO/ © PHIL SHELDON)

Q. When Bill Clinton tripped over a step exiting Greg Norman's house during a visit there in 1997, who happened to be in the right place at the right time to catch the president?

A. The Shark himself.

Q. What was the final-round score Nick Faldo shot to win the 1996 Masters over Norman?

A. 67.

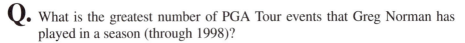

Q. What is the greatest number of PGA Tour events that Greg Norman has played in a season (through 1998)?

A. Nineteen. Even with such a limited schedule, Norman has notched nine top-ten finishes on the money list.

Q. On what British Open venue in 1976 did Seve Ballesteros first serve notice of his impending greatness by tying Jack Nicklaus for second place, behind winner Johnny Miller?

A. Royal Birkdale.

Q. Greg Norman sat out much of the 1998 season for what health-related reason?

A. Shoulder surgery.

Q. Nick Faldo's reputation as "Robogolfer" was secured when he won the 1987 British Open by performing what feat of consistency on the final day?

A. He made eighteen consecutive pars.

Q. How many top-ten money-list finishes on the PGA Tour has Seve Ballesteros had?

A. None, mostly because he has played only a handful of American events. His best money-list finish was eighteenth in 1983.

Q. Greg Norman was once guest pilot of what kind of military aircraft normally launched from aircraft carriers?

A. The navy's F-14 Tomcat.

Q. How did Seve Ballesteros do in his first tournament appearance as a professional?

A. He opened with an 89 at the 1974 Portuguese Open and bolted, in tears.

Q. Where does Seve reside these days?

A. Monaco.

This might have been the last time anyone ever saw **Seve Ballesteros** smiling after finishing second. The occasion is the 1976 British Open posttournament ceremony, with Seve, still a teenager, being introduced as a joint runner-up (with Jack Nicklaus) behind champion Johnny Miller, seen seated in the middle. Seated on the left is Mark James, who more than two decades later would succeed Seve as European Ryder Cup captain for the 1999 Matches. (© PHIL SHELDON)

Q. Nick Faldo was the first golfer ever to break 200 for the first three rounds of what major tournament?

A. The British Open, where in 1990 he opened 67, 65, 67 for a 199 three-day total en route to a five-shot victory over Payne Stewart and Mark McNulty.

Q. Why was Greg Norman disqualified from the 1996 Greater Hartford Open?

A. He played a type of Maxfli ball sent him by the company that wasn't on the USGA's list of approved golf balls.

Q. Seve Ballesteros started playing golf at the age of seven using the clubhead of what club, fastened to a shaft whittled from a stick?

A. Three-iron.

Q. Which two events on the PGA Tour schedule has Seve won twice each?

A. The Masters and the Manufacturers Hanover Westchester Classic, the latter now known simply as the Buick Classic.

Q. Greg Norman ended about seven months of no golf following 1998 shoulder surgery by returning to competition and immediately winning what event?

A. His own Franklin Templeton Shark Shootout, while partnered with Steve Elkington.

Q. Simultaneously with Norman's return to the winner's circle in 1998, Nick Faldo was teaming with what golfer to lead England to its first-ever victory in the World Cup of Golf?

A. David Carter.

Q. When Greg Norman jumped back atop the world rankings in 1994, he ended what rival's record eighty-one-week stay at the top?

A. Nick Faldo.

Q. What 400-acre island off the coast of Ireland did Nick Faldo reportedly pay £1 million to purchase?

A. Bartragh.

Q. What 1992 Formula One world champion race-car driver is one of Greg Norman's good buddies and a Florida neighbor?

A. Nigel Mansell.

Nick Faldo and **Greg Norman** embrace on the eighteenth green at Augusta, where Faldo has just completed a comeback victory over a faltering Norman at the 1996 Masters.

(© PHIL SHELDON)

Q. In what English county was Nick Faldo born?

A. Hertfordshire.

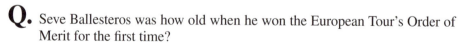

Q. Seve Ballesteros was how old when he won the European Tour's Order of Merit for the first time?

A. Nineteen, in 1976.

Q. Nick Faldo briefly attended what American university in the seventies?

A. University of Houston.

Q. What are the names of Seve Ballesteros's three older brothers?

A. Baldomero, Manuel, and Vicente.

Q. In what year did Nick Faldo win the European Order of Merit for the first time?

A. 1983.

Q. What is the timing irony of Greg Norman's three PGA Tour money titles and three Vardon Trophy triumphs?

A. He has never won both in the same year.

Q. What was Greg Norman's winning score in the 1993 British Open, which set the record for low scoring in a major?

A. 267.

Q. Seve Ballesteros's first PGA Tour victory came in what event?

A. The Greater Greensboro Open, in 1978.

Q. In what year did Nick Faldo emerge as the European Tour's Rookie of the Year?

A. 1977.

Q. What four European superstars of the 1980s, major-tournament winners all, were born within eleven months of Seve Ballesteros?

A. Nick Faldo, Ian Woosnam, Sandy Lyle, and Bernhard Langer.

Q. What was Norman's first play-off loss in the United States?

A. To Mike Nicolette in the 1983 Bay Hill Classic.

17

SCORECARD

50 Questions
Par: 4

Correct answers	Score	
48–50	Eagle	2
35–47	Birdie	3
25–34	Par	4
15–24	Bogey	5
10–14	Double Bogey	6
Less than 10	Triple Bogey	7

Your score _____

Q. What former NFL quarterback was the first golfer to send in his entry form to qualify for the 1996 U.S. Open?

A. Phil Simms.

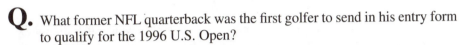

Q. With what fellow Senior Tour golfer did Dave Hill once duke it out at a golf event?

A. J. C. Snead.

Q. As reported by *Sports Illustrated* in 1998, what golfing old-timer had the gall to take Tiger Woods to task for occasional outbursts of anger on the golf course?

A. "Terrible" Tommy Bolt, one of golf's all-time human volcanoes.

Q. What was the original name of the "minor league" golf circuit that later got a new sponsor and became known as the Nike Tour?

A. The Ben Hogan Tour, which started play in 1990.

Q. What survivor of prostate cancer returned to the Senior PGA Tour and picked up where he left off, winning the Transamerica and more than $1 million in 1998?

A. Jim Colbert.

Q. What longtime club pro chucked his anonymity by winning the 1993 PGA Seniors' Championship?

A. Tom Wargo.

Q. In what city was the World Golf Village and Hall of Fame opened in 1998?

A. St. Augustine, Florida.

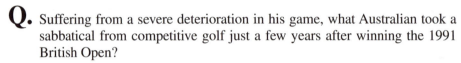

Q. Suffering from a severe deterioration in his game, what Australian took a sabbatical from competitive golf just a few years after winning the 1991 British Open?

A. Ian Baker-Finch.

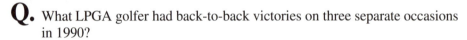

Q. What former Ryder Cupper ended his streak of forty-six missed cuts by making it to the weekend at the 1998 Greater Milwaukee Open?

A. Chip Beck.

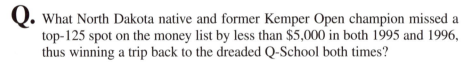

Q. What LPGA golfer had back-to-back victories on three separate occasions in 1990?

A. Beth Daniel.

Q. What North Dakota native and former Kemper Open champion missed a top-125 spot on the money list by less than $5,000 in both 1995 and 1996, thus winning a trip back to the dreaded Q-School both times?

A. Tom Byrum.

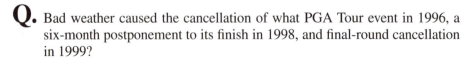

Q. Bad weather caused the cancellation of what PGA Tour event in 1996, a six-month postponement to its finish in 1998, and final-round cancellation in 1999?

A. The AT&T Pebble Beach National Pro-Am.

Q. In 1997 who became the first American tour golfer to top the $2 million mark in a year's earnings?

A. Hale Irwin, nosing out Tiger Woods by a matter of weeks.

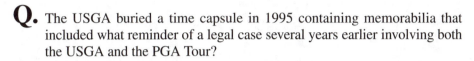

Q. The USGA buried a time capsule in 1995 containing memorabilia that included what reminder of a legal case several years earlier involving both the USGA and the PGA Tour?

A. Ping Eye2 irons, owned by Bob Gilder, one of the tour players involved in the famous square-grooves issue.

Q. Tom Watson ended a nine-year victory drought in America by winning what 1996 event?

A. The Memorial Tournament.

Q. What popular and good-natured PGA Tour golfer and winner of four tour events, including the 1992 Buick Open, has struggled with epilepsy in recent years?

A. Dan Forsman.

Q. In the late 1990s what renowned golf psychologist signed a deal with Chrysler?

A. Bob Rotella.

Q. What former University of Maryland golf coach won five PGA Tour events between 1991 and 1998?

A. Fred Funk.

When golf fans and his fellow competitors see **Tiger Woods** coming out with the clenched fist, as he is starting to do here at the 1998 Johnnie Walker World Championship, you can bet the fat lady is about to sing.

(© PHIL SHELDON)

Q. What former club pro died of lung cancer less than a year after reaching the zenith of his competitive career by winning the 1997 Senior Players Championship?

A. Larry Gilbert.

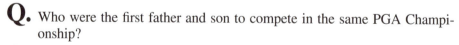

Q. Who were the first father and son to compete in the same PGA Championship?

A. Al and Brent Geiberger, in 1998.

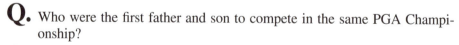

Q. In a rainy play-off for the 1997 season-opening Mercedes Championship, who did Tiger Woods beat?

A. Tom Lehman.

Q. Who was the first golfer to break 190 in the first three rounds of a PGA Tour event?

A. John Cook, who opened the 1996 FedEx St. Jude Classic with rounds of 64, 62, and 63 (189).

Q. By how much was Billy Andrade nudged out of the final money-list spot for the 1997 Tour Championship?

A. Five bucks, by Andrew Magee, who was thirtieth.

Q. Who was the first man to win on the regular PGA Tour and the Senior PGA Tour in the same calendar year?

A. Raymond Floyd, who won the Doral Ryder Open as well as three Senior Tour events in 1992 after turning fifty in September.

Q. What three golfers barely escaped serious injury when the driver of the courtesy car they were riding in at the 1997 Texas Open collapsed at the wheel with a heart attack, sending the car out of control at speeds up to eighty miles per hour before the players managed to bring it to a stop?

A. Brad Bryant, Mark Calcavecchia, and Mark Weibe (as in "We be scared, man").

Q. When was the last time a big-hitting recovering alcoholic with a penchant for shaving his head won a tournament classified as a major?

A. 1998, when Hank Kuehne won the U.S. Amateur. (If you answered John Daly, penalize yourself a stroke.)

Q. What journeyman pro golfer didn't crack the top 100 on the PGA Tour money list until he was forty-four and didn't win a tour event until 1995 at age forty-seven?

A. Ed Dougherty.

Q. What PGA Championship winner of the 1990s is also an accomplished caricaturist?

A. Steve Elkington.

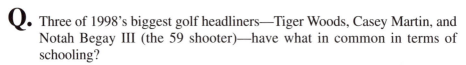

Q. Who was the first player to crack the $200,000 mark in a Nike Tour season?

A. Stewart Cink, in 1996.

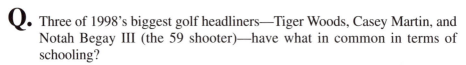

Q. Three of 1998's biggest golf headliners—Tiger Woods, Casey Martin, and Notah Begay III (the 59 shooter)—have what in common in terms of schooling?

A. All played golf at Stanford.

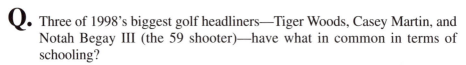

Q. Who is the only lefty other than Phil Mickelson to have won a PGA Tour event in the nineties?

A. Russ Cochran, at the 1991 Centel Western Open.

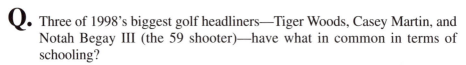

Q. It took how many events for Tiger Woods to become the fastest player to the $1 million mark?

A. Nine, between late 1996 and early 1997.

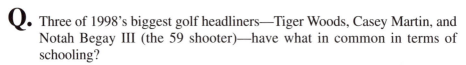

Q. Consistent with his days as a football player, 1992 Senior Tour rookie Harry Toscano stood out that year as the only tour player to wear what on his face?

A. Eye-black.

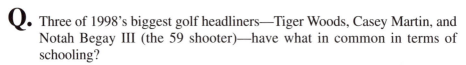

Q. When Lee Janzen won U.S. Opens in 1993 and 1998, who finished second both times?

A. Payne Stewart.

Q. What big-hitting Brit bought a Ferrari 456 sports car in 1996 at the age of thirty-two, saying, "I wanted to have five or six years in it when I didn't look stupid"?

A. Laura Davies.

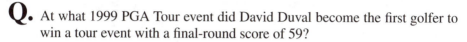

Q. At what 1999 PGA Tour event did David Duval become the first golfer to win a tour event with a final-round score of 59?

A. The Bob Hope Chrysler Classic.

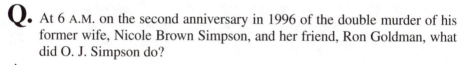

Q. At 6 A.M. on the second anniversary in 1996 of the double murder of his former wife, Nicole Brown Simpson, and her friend, Ron Goldman, what did O. J. Simpson do?

A. Teed off for a round of golf at Griffith Park in Los Angeles.

Q. In what PGA Tour event did Tiger Woods earn his first victory as a pro?

A. The 1996 Las Vegas Invitational.

Q. What PGA Tour golfer and former Ryder Cupper, whose career started going to the pits in the mid-1990s, resorted to using his son's twenty-six-inch putter for a while?

A. Ken Green.

Q. Whose record of nine Senior PGA Tour victories in one season did Hale Irwin tie in 1997?

A. Peter Thomson's, set in 1985.

Q. After suffering earlier in the year from walking pneumonia and then Bell's palsy, which temporarily paralyzed the right side of his face, what golfer won the 1996 Canon Greater Hartford Open?

A. D. A. Weibring.

Iron Byrum

When it comes to agonizing over the annual top-125 cut-off for the PGA Tour exemption list, no one in the 1990s knows the agony of defeat better than brothers **Tom** and **Curt Byrum**. Start with Tom: In both 1995 and 1996, the former Kemper Open champion ended up less than $5,000 away from one of the coveted 125 spots. Miss out, and a golfer ends up back in Q-School, roughly the equivalent of getting a different tooth filled on six consecutive days—without Novocain. Then there's Curt, who suffered through the ultimate top-125 tearjerker in 1994. On the top-125 bubble going into that year's last full-field event, the Las Vegas Invitational, Byrum breathed a huge sigh of relief when he made the cut. All he had to do now was finish the tournament, and last-place money would be good enough to make the top 125. With only three holes to go on Sunday, Curt Byrum stepped to the sixteenth tee and hit a drive that looked like it might be lost. No problem; Byrum immediately re-teed and hit a provisional. Byrum found his first ball, but it was in an unplayable lie. Surveying the lay of the land, he opted to return to the tee, take a penalty stroke for the unplayable lie and, as allowed by the rules, hit another drive with his original ball. By this time, however, the group behind Byrum—Phil Mickelson and Michael Allen—had arrived at the sixteenth and hit their tee shots. Byrum teed it up and knocked his third stroke into the fairway. Then the unthinkable happened. Byrum then hit Allen's ball by mistake, a grievous error he didn't discover until after he had holed out and subsequently teed off on the next hole. Under the Rules of Golf, Byrum was disqualified because he had started his next hole of play before realizing his violation. Rules officials at the scene tried in vain to find a loophole that would allow Byrum to finish the tournament. PGA Tour rules allowed him to keep the last-place money, but it couldn't count as official money. Unbelievably, he had fallen out of the top 125. Byrum was inconsolable. There's a happy ending to this story, however. When José Maria Olazábal announced later that fall he wouldn't exercise his top-125 exemption for the next year, 1995, that opened up a spot for Byrum. Tour-exemption salvation was his.

Q. What "middle of the packer" had a breakthrough year in 1990 with four PGA Tour victories and more than $1 million in earnings?

A. Wayne Levi.

Q. From how many strokes back did Justin Leonard come to win the 1997 British Open with a closing 65?

A. Five.

Q. Who replaced David Graham as captain of the International team for the 1996 Presidents Cup after Graham's awkward ouster in a players' coup?

A. Peter Thomson.

Q. How far was Gil Morgan past his fiftieth birthday in 1996 when he became the youngest winner of a Senior PGA Tour event?

A. Eleven days.

Q. How did a last-minute sponsor's exemption to the 1996 Friendly's Classic literally save golfer Charlotta Sorenstam's life?

A. She was scheduled to fly the unfriendly skies to Paris on TWA Flight 800, which exploded in midair, killing all 228 aboard.

Q. What father-son duo combined to top the $3 million mark for official 1998 earnings on their respective tours?

A. Bob Duval on the Senior PGA Tour; son David Duval on the flat-belly circuit.

Q. The Executive Women's Golf League was founded in 1991 by whom?

A. Nancy Oliver.

Ten Tournament Champions of the 1990s Who Are Living Proof You Don't Have to Grow Up with a Twelve-Month Tan to Be a Successful Golfer

Golfer	Native Home	Biggest 1990s Victory
Patty Sheehan	Vermont	1992, 1994 U.S. Women's Open
Tom Lehman	Minnesota	1996 British Open
Sherri Steinhauer	Wisconsin	1992 du Maurier Classic
Fred Couples	Washington	1992 Masters
Annika Sorenstam	Sweden	1995, 1996 U.S. Women's Open
Jeff Sluman	New York	1997 Tucson Chrysler Classic
Kris Tschetter	South Dakota	1992 Northgate Computer Classic
Paul Azinger	Massachusetts	1993 PGA Championship
Dawn Coe-Jones	British Columbia	1995 Chrysler-Plymouth Tournament of Champions
Jay Don Blake	Utah	1991 Shearson Lehman Brothers Open

Q. Who finally prevailed as the winner of the 1998 AT&T Pebble Beach National Pro-Am, the finish of which was delayed more than six months because of cruddy weather?

A. Phil Mickelson.

———

Q. A career doubleheader sweep of the U.S. Open and U.S. Senior Open was most recently accomplished by whom?

A. Hale Irwin, who joined that select fraternity by winning the 1998 Senior Open.

———

Q. Whose first PGA Tour victory came in a six-man play-off at the 1996 Byron Nelson Classic?

A. Neal Lancaster.

Q. What was Tiger Woods's best finish in a "professional" major before he turned pro?

A. Tie for twenty-second at the 1996 British Open.

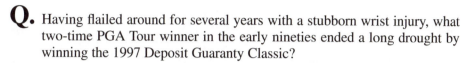

Q. Having flailed around for several years with a stubborn wrist injury, what two-time PGA Tour winner in the early nineties ended a long drought by winning the 1997 Deposit Guaranty Classic?

A. Billy Ray Brown.

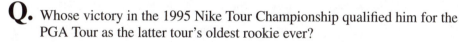

Q. Whose victory in the 1995 Nike Tour Championship qualified him for the PGA Tour as the latter tour's oldest rookie ever?

A. Allen Doyle, who was forty-seven at the time.

Q. The winning bid of almost $750,000 for JFK's golf bag and clubs was made at a 1996 auction by what celebrity?

A. Arnold Schwarzenegger.

Q. Current Senior PGA Tour golfer Frank Conner was a standout in what other sport?

A. Tennis. Conner twice competed in tennis's U.S. Open during the sixties.

Q. Tiger Woods defeated what three golfers in the finals when he ran the table in the U.S. Amateur in 1994, 1995, and 1996?

A. Trip Kuehne, Buddy Marucci Jr., and Steve Scott, respectively.

Q. What former starting cornerback for Vince Lombardi's Green Bay Packers made it into the field for the 1996 U.S. Senior Open, although he missed the cut?

A. Jesse Whittenton.

Q. What first-time PGA Tour winner in 1996 won that year's BellSouth Classic the week after he had won a Nike Tour event?

A. Paul Stankowski.

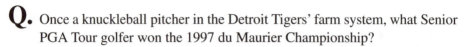

Q. Once a knuckleball pitcher in the Detroit Tigers' farm system, what Senior PGA Tour golfer won the 1997 du Maurier Championship?

A. Jack Kiefer.

Q. Cart-riding Casey Martin won what Nike Tour event in early 1998?

A. The Lakeland Classic.

Q. What Olympic gold-medal skier pulled out of the 1997 Italian Open pro-am when he learned he wasn't going to get an appearance fee?

A. Alberto Tomba.

Q. What golf club was poised to be the venue for golf as a resurrected Olympics sport at the 1996 Summer Games before that idea was snuffed out, apparently for political reasons?

A. Augusta National.

Q. What veteran golfer, after leaving the tour for a number of years to coach golf at the University of Houston, returned to competition in 1994 with a bang by quickly winning two Nike Tour events?

A. Keith Fergus.

Q. Who was the USGA's first female president, elected to the position in 1995?

A. Judy Bell.

Until 1998 rolled around, **Mark O'Meara** was one of about two or three guys playing hot potato with the moniker of "Best Golfer Never to Have Won a Major." O'Meara's main claim to fame was winning at Pebble Beach about every other year, it seemed. Then in 1998, he not only broke through in the majors' column by winning at Augusta, he followed up three months later by beating fellow American Brian Watts to win the 1998 British Open, which is where he's shown here. As for that aforementioned moniker, 1999 began with the likes of Colin Montgomerie and Phil Mickelson wearing the albatross around their necks. (JAN TRAYLEN PHOTO/© PHIL SHELDON)

Q. Suspicion regarding O. J. Simpson's alibi in his double-murder trial only grew when he gave what dubious golf-related account of his activities around the time of the murders?

A. That he had been in his backyard "chipping" with a fairway wood. (The sixty-degree wedge, we presume, is for those 200-yard carries over water.)

Q. What double winner of the 1990 Players Championship and Nabisco (Tour) Championships had all but retired to his Kentucky horse farm by the end of the decade?

A. Jodie Mudd.

Q. What golf coach with an NFL Hall of Fame pedigree built Jackson State University into a golf powerhouse of the 1990s?

A. Eddie Payton, Walter's brother.

Q. What two Nike Tour players in 1998 shot 59s in official competition?

A. Notah Begay III and Doug Dunakey.

Q. Who was the PGA Tour rookie in 1990 who holed out a seven-iron from 176 yards at the Nestlé Invitational to nick at the wire—you guessed it—Greg Norman?

A. Robert Gamez.

Q. In 1996 what pro football star was docked two strokes for missing his starting time at his own celebrity tournament?

A. Dan Marino.

Q. What political office has Rocky Thompson, a colorful Senior PGA Tour mainstay of the nineties, held for many years?

A. Mayor of Toco, Texas.

Q. What insect-borne affliction did a number on golfer Tim Simpson's career, knocking him for a loop in the early nineties while his condition went undiagnosed for about two years?

A. Lyme disease.

Q. Billy Andrade has partnered with what baseball star and longtime buddy in the AT&T Pebble Beach National Pro-Am?

A. Mark McGwire.

———— ∞ ————

Q. What Texas cattle farmer came out of nowhere to qualify for the 1995 Senior PGA Tour and then to write a book called *Greener Pastures*?

A. Robert Landers.

———— ∞ ————

Q. Tiger Woods was once involved in what criminal act that took place outside his Stanford University dorm?

A. He was mugged.

———— ∞ ————

Q. Steve Jones won the 1996 U.S. Open several years after severely injuring a finger in what kind of accident that nearly ended his career?

A. Jones flipped a dirt bike.

———— ∞ ————

Q. Paul Azinger's memorable blast-in from a greenside bunker at the 1993 Memorial Tournament gave him a one-shot victory over whom?

A. Corey Pavin.

———— ∞ ————

Q. Who was the first golfer to jump his official PGA Tour earnings by more than $1 million from one year to the next?

A. Billy Mayfair, who went from about $158,000 in 1994 to more than $1.5 million in 1995.

———— ∞ ————

Q. Whose stirring victory at Pebble Beach in 1994 made him one of the select few ever to win the same event in three different decades?

A. Johnny Miller, who also won there in 1974 and 1987.

18

SCORECARD

80 Questions
Par: 5

Correct answers	Score	
78–80	Double eagle	2
70–77	Eagle	3
55–69	Birdie	4
40–54	Par	5
25–39	Bogey	6
15–24	Double Bogey	7
Less than 15	Triple Bogey	8

Your score _____

RESOURCES

Barkow, Al. *The History of the PGA Tour.* New York: Doubleday, 1989.

Burnett, Jim. *Tee Times.* New York: A Lisa Drew Book/Scribner, 1997.

Campbell, Malcolm. *The Random House International Encyclopedia of Golf.* New York: Random House, 1991.

Christian, Frank Jr., and Cal Brown. *Augusta National and the Masters: A Photographer's Scrapbook.* Chelsea, Michigan: Sleeping Bear Press, 1996.

Dobereiner, Peter. *Golf Rules Explained.* Great Britain: David and Charles, 1996.

Donovan, Richard E., and Joseph S. F. Murdoch. *The Game of Golf and the Printed Word, 1566–1985.* Endicott, New York: Castalio Press, 1988.

Eubanks, Steve. *Augusta.* Nashville, Tennessee: Rutledge Hill Press, 1997.

Golf Digest (1990–1998)

Golf Magazine (1990–1998)

Golf Magazine's Encyclopedia of Golf. New York: HarperCollins, 1993.

Golf World (1985–1998)

Gregston, Gene. *Hogan: The Man Who Played for Glory.* Grass Valley, California: Booklegger, 1990.

Guest, Larry. *Arnie: Inside the Legend.* Orlando, Florida: Tribune Publishing, 1993.

Hagen, Walter. *The Walter Hagen Story.* New York: Simon and Schuster, 1956.

Hobbs, Michael. *In Celebration of Golf.* New York: Charles Scribner's Sons, 1983.

Jenkins, Dan. *The Dogged Victims of Inexorable Fate.* New York: Little, Brown, and Company/Sports Illustrated, 1970.

Jones, Robert T. Jr., and O. B. Keeler. *Down the Fairway.* New York: Minton, Balch, and Company, 1927.

Loeffelbein, Bob. *Offbeat Golf.* Santa Monica, California: Santa Monica Press, 1998.

LPGA Media Guide, 1998.

Matuz, Roger. *Inside Sports Golf.* Detroit, Michigan: Visible Ink Press, 1997.

McCord, Gary, with John Huggan. *Golf for Dummies.* Foster City, California: IDG Books Worldwide, 1996.

McCormack, Mark. *Arnie.* New York: Simon and Schuster, 1967.

McCormack, Mark. *The World of Professional Golf 1997.* IMG Publishing, 1997.

McDonnell, Michael. *Golf: The Great Ones.* New York: Drake Publishers, 1971.

Nelson, Byron. *How I Played the Game.* Dallas: Taylor, 1993.

————. *Byron Nelson's Little Black Book.* Arlington, Texas: The Summit Group, 1995.

Peper, George, and the editors of Golf Magazine. *Golf in America.* New York: Harry Abrams, 1994.

PGA Tour Media Guide, 1998.

Sampson, Curt. *Hogan.* Nashville, Tennessee: Rutledge Hill Press, 1996.

————. *The Masters.* New York: Villard, 1998.

Scott, Tom, and Geoffrey Cousins. *The Golf Immortals.* New York: Hart, 1969.

Senior PGA Tour Media Guide, 1998.

Shaw, Mark. *Nicklaus.* Dallas, Texas: Taylor, 1997.

Sifford, Charlie, with James Gullo. *Just Let Me Play.* Latham, New York: British American Publishing, 1992.

Snead, Sam, with Fran Pirozzolo. *The Game I Love.* New York: Ballantine Books, 1997.

Waggoner, Glen. *Divots, Shanks, Gimmes, Mulligans, and Chili Dips.* New York: Villard, 1993.

About the Author

Mike Towle has been a correspondent for *Golf World* and *Golf Illustrated* magazines, and covered golf as a staff writer for the *Fort Worth Star-Telegram* and *The National Sports Daily*. Towle coauthored *Golf and ADA: A Winning Twosome* with Greg Jones, authored *True Champions,* and has edited numerous golf books including *Byron Nelson's Little Black Book* and *Hogan* by Curt Sampson. Towle, a Vermont native and Notre Dame graduate, lives in Nashville, Tennessee, with his wife, Holley, and son, Andrew.